MW00574777

WEAPON

GERMAN AUTOMATIC RIFLES 1941–45

CHRIS McNAB

Series Editor Martin Pegler

First published in Great Britain in 2013 by Osprey Publishing,
Midland House, West Way, Botley, Oxford, OX2 0PH, UK
43-01 21st Street, Suite 220B, Long Island City, NY 11101, USA
E-mail: info@ospreypublishing.com

Osprey Publishing is part of the Osprey Group

A CIP catalogue record for this book is available from the British
Library

Print ISBN: 978 1 78096 385 3
PDF ebook ISBN: 978 1 78096 386 0
ePub ebook ISBN: 978 1 78096 387 7

Index by Judy Oliver
Typeset in Sabon and Univers
Battlescenes by Ramiro Bujeiro
Cutaway by Alan Gilliland
Originated by PDQ Media, Bungay, UK
Printed in China through Worldprint Ltd

13 14 15 16 17   10 9 8 7 6 5 4 3 2 1

Osprey Publishing is supporting the Woodland Trust, the UK's
leading woodland conservation charity, by funding the dedication
of trees.

Author's acknowledgements

I would like to thank several people for their help and support in
producing this book. Special thanks go to Chuck Norton, Joseph
Magers and Claus Espeholt for generously providing many of the
weapons photos. I would also like to thank the Osprey team –
Nick Reynolds, Tom Milner and series editor Martin Pegler – for
diligently raising all the right questions.

Author's note

In the title of this book, and on occasions in the text, the word
'automatic' is used as shorthand for both semi- and full-auto
weapons. This usage has become common currency in writing
about firearms, but when it raises the potential for confusion
I clearly distinguish between semi- and full-auto fire.

Artist's note

Readers may care to note that the original paintings from which
the battlescenes in this book were prepared are available for
private sale. All reproduction copyright whatsoever is retained
by the Publishers. All inquiries should be addressed to:

Ramiro Bujeiro, C.C. 28, 1602 Florida, Argentina

The Publishers regret that they can enter into no correspondence
upon this matter.

Editor's note

1km = 0.62 miles
1m = 3.28ft
1cm = 0.39in
1kg = 2.20lb
1m/sec = 3.28ft/sec

www.ospreypublishing.com

CONTENTS

INTRODUCTION

There is no denying that the bolt-action rifle changed the face of warfare. From its origins in the 1830s until the end of World War II (1939–45), the bolt-action rifle became the defining firearm of most of the world's modern armies (the United States became a forward-thinking exception with its adoption of the M1 Garand from 1936). It offered an enduring battlefield package. Weapons such as the 7.92mm Mauser Gewehr 98, the .303in Short Magazine Lee-Enfield and the .30-06-calibre Springfield M1903 were resilient, powerful, generally easy to handle and could be frighteningly accurate to long ranges – in the trenches of World War I, exposing just a fraction of skull above the trench parapet would likely result in death by head-shot from an opposing sniper.

Yet for all the undeniable merits of the bolt-action rifle, by the end of World War I (1914–18) most combatant nations were as aware of the weapon's limitations as its benefits. The guns were long, heavy and cumbersome, not least in the dynamic horrors of close-quarters trench combat, where a rifle measuring 1,255mm (in the case of the Gew 98) was awkward to wield with speed against multiple targets. The operating mechanism – the manual working of a bolt system – was a world of improvement over the arm-aching days of muzzle-loading, but it was still sluggish when fleeting enemies had to be engaged instinctively. (Maximum rate of fire for a well-trained rifleman with a smooth-running gun was about 15rpm.) Furthermore, many began to question the actual value of the rifle's reach. A potent cartridge such as the 7.92×57mm Mauser or 8×50mmR Lebel could kill targets the shooter could scarcely see, let alone hit, unless using expensive visual accessories such as telescopic sights. In fact, German combat studies in the 1920s (about which more later) suggested that most actual combat took place at ranges of around or below 300m, meaning that the shoulder-bruising thump of the full-power rifle round, and the arcing flight of the bullet towards the distant horizon, were generally unnecessary.

For these reasons, the bolt-action rifle was, during the first half of the 20th century, largely sandwiched between two types of firearm in an army – the submachine gun and the machine gun. The submachine gun, a full-auto weapon firing pistol-calibre ammunition, gave short-range (up to about 150m) rapid firepower ideally suited to close-quarters combat. The machine gun, by contrast, dealt out long-range attrition using a broad 'beaten zone' of fire and a rate of fire that even multiple riflemen could not hope to match. The bolt-action rifle remained in the middle ground – redoubtable, powerful, functional and ubiquitous.

There was, however, another way forward for the rifle. Within years of the birth of automatic firepower, courtesy of Hiram Maxim's recoil-powered machine gun in 1883, resourceful minds were looking at ways in which to apply the principles of self-loading to rifles. (The advent of bulky self-loading handguns such as the Borchardt *Selbstladepistol* of 1893 had at least proved that semi-automatic principles could be applied to hand-held firearms.) The original innovators in this regard were the Mexican Manuel Mondragón and the appropriately named Danish inventor Soren H. Bang. During the 1890s and the early years of the 20th century, both gunmakers developed weapons that used propellant gas to cycle the weapon through loading, firing, extraction and ejection, the cycle being performed each time the trigger was pulled. The Bang rifles (he developed several such firearms) used a system in which a muzzle cone caught the propellant gas on firing. The gas in turn pushed the cone forward and worked an operating rod attached to the bolt mechanism, unlocking and retracting the bolt and performing the ejection and reloading cycle. The Bang system was not a commercial success; his rifles were unreliable and complex, and so never went into production. They are significant for our study here, however, because the Bang principle actually went on to inform the German Gew 41 automatic rifles.

The Mondragón rifle utilized a different, and more visionary, method of operation. It applied the gas-operation system still fundamental (with much variation) to many of the world's automatic rifles and light

A German soldier sits at his post on the Eastern Front in 1942. Stacked in front of him are Kar 98k bolt-action rifles, the standard firearm of the Wehrmacht in World War II. German experiments in automatic rifles aimed to transform the firepower of the individual rifleman. (BArch, Bild 101I-394-1459-16, Wanderer, W.)

machine guns. Propellant gas was tapped off from the barrel to mechanically unlock the bolt and power it to the rear against the recoil spring. The bolt was of a rotating type, lugs on the bolt head locking into projections to the rear of the breech, and it rotated through its locking/unlocking motion via projections on the cocking handle engaging with helical grooves in the bolt body. Almost in acknowledgement that the world's military community did not quite yet trust semi-automatic weaponry, the Mondragón rifle's gas system could be disconnected from the bolt system, converting the firearm back into a conventional straight-pull bolt-action rifle.

Although the later M1 Garand rifle would be the world's first standard-issue semi-auto rifle, the 7×57mm Mondragón was nevertheless one of the first actually to enter military service, with the Mexican Army in 1908. It was not a production success, however, despite commercial realities forcing it into manufacture with the capable SIG (Schweizerische Industrie Gesellschaft) firm, of Switzerland. Just 400 weapons were actually in the hands of the Mexican forces by 1911 (of 4,000 ordered), and SIG was left with about 1,000 unsold guns in stock. Interestingly, in 1915 SIG's Mondragón rifles were purchased by the fledgling German air force, modified to 30-round helical 'snail' magazines (they had previous fired from eight-round clip-loaded magazines) and issued as self-defence weapons to the aviators. The rigours of wartime service were not kind to the fragile Mondragón, so they were rather quickly withdrawn from front-line service. Yet Manuel Mondragón's legacy remained in his essentially sound principles of gas-operated weaponry.

The sheer cost of a semi-auto weapon compared to a bolt-action rifle, especially in moments of wartime exigency, meant that semi-auto weapons were an expensive diversion. The period from 1900 to 1918 nevertheless saw a steady expansion in the number of semi-automatic weapons in soldiers' hands, although often on an experimental basis, and always in limited numbers. The French company Manufacture d'Armes de Saint-Etienne produced the RSC Modèle 1917, an ineffectual and ugly gas-operated rifle chambered for the 8×50mmR Lebel. More interesting was the 6.5×52mm Cei-Rigotti (named after the eponymous captain responsible), an Italian self-loading carbine actually developed in 1900. This futuristic weapon was gas-operated via a short-stroke piston system, the rotating bolt featuring two lugs that locked into recesses in the barrel extension. Not only could it fire from 10-, 20- or even 50-round detachable magazines, but it was also history's first selective-fire weapon – a selector switch allowed the user to choose between semi-auto and full-auto fire. No one saw past the Cei-Rigotti's teething troubles, so the weapon was another commercial failure, although the fact that carbines such as the US M1 later used a similar system hints at its importance.

The Americans themselves had a rather uneven relationship with the automatic rifle during World War I. In 1917–18, Remington designer John Pedersen invented a bizarre-looking attachment that in a much-publicized 15 seconds (the reality was far longer in combat conditions) could convert a bolt-action Springfield M1903 rifle into a blowback-operated semi-automatic rifle. Some 65,000 Pedersen Devices were manufactured by war's end, but practical trials showed it to be ill-suited to battlefield use and insufficiently reliable.

This could not be said for another American invention, the Browning Automatic Rifle (BAR). Invented by John Browning, this .30-calibre firearm showed the full potential of the gas-operated system in a solid weapon that sat somewhere in role between heavy rifle and light machine gun. It could fire on full-auto at a rate of 350 or 550rpm; in fact, its early single-shot capability was dropped in favour of just two full-auto rates (although some Marine Corps units later modified the gun back to offer single-shot mode). Reliability was its major virtue, but it fell short of perfection owing to its awkward weight and size and the limitation of its 20-round magazine. Nevertheless, the BAR remained in service with US forces until the 1950s, and proved that gas-operated weapons offered a solid way forward in automatic firepower.

Germany was by no means left out of the early experimentation with semi-auto rifles. In fact, the ever-inventive Mauser concern secured patents in 1898 for the c/98 short-recoil rifle. (In short recoil, the barrel and bolt recoil locked together for less than the length of a cartridge before unlocking, whereas in long recoil the components only unlock once they have travelled more than the length of a cartridge case.) Despite its trial among the German Army in 1901, the c/98 never went beyond prototype models, and Mauser's subsequent three attempts to perfect a recoil-operated rifle were largely unsuccessful. The final version, the Aviator's Rifle Model 16, was used again in unimpressive numbers by the German air force, and by a few quickly disillusioned infantrymen, but by the end of the war the self-loading rifle had largely failed to show its promise, at least in Europe. The journey was not over yet for Germany, however, and it continued to sow seeds even in the unpromising soil of the interwar years.

DEVELOPMENT
Beyond bolt-action

From 1919, the restrictive grip placed around Germany's armed services by the Versailles Treaty was tight indeed. The Reichswehr (German Army) became little more than a national security force, and strict limitations were placed on both the types and numbers of weapons in circulation. Yet if the 1920s and 1930s proved anything, it was that German determination to circumvent the terms of the treaty was greater than the victors' persistence in enforcing them. Much technological investment went underground, and automatic-rifle development was no exception.

Driving the experimentation in automatic rifles was the continuing interest in producing a rifle adapted to more realistic combat ranges, based on an 'intermediate' cartridge somewhere between a full-power rifle round and pistol cartridge. A landmark event in this process was a meeting of the Inspektion der Infanterie (Inspectorate of Infantry) and Inspektion der Kavallerie (Inspectorate of Cavalry) with the Inspektion für Waffen und Gerät (Inspectorate for Weapons and Equipment) in June 1921. Among the topics for discussion were the merits and problems of several different types of new cartridge, including caseless and aluminium types, and there was some soul-searching about the failures of previous self-loading rifles, as firearms historians Guus de Vries and Bas J. Martens have noted:

> The record explains that previous trials with self-loading rifles had not been successful, due to the great recoil force of the S-cartridge [the standard round of the German Mauser Gew 98 rifle]. What was needed, most of those present agreed, was a weapon with a high rate

of fire, a shorter cartridge, and an effective range of up to 800 meters. The whole was quite neatly summarized by *Oberleutnant* von Dittelberger, who stated that the desire for 'rapid automatic fire will lead to an improved submachine gun with better small-calibre ammunition'. (de Vries & Martens 2003: 10)

The relatively informal discussion in 1921 steadily coalesced into more officially stated aims. A memorandum issued by the Inspektion der Infanterie in January 1923 outlined the requirement for a selective-fire weapon with a 20- or 30-round magazine capacity, and an optimal combat performance at ranges of up to 400m. Although this memorandum by no means amounted to an official competition or commission, both private and state-funded gunmakers began to play around with the automatic concept. The explorations began to gather pace during the 1930s, once Germany had effectively publicly rejected the Versailles limitations in favour of Hitler's massive rearmament programme.

Some manufacturers – including IWG, Rheinmetall and Mauser – chose to stick with the 7.92×57mm cartridge, rather than reinvent the ammunition.

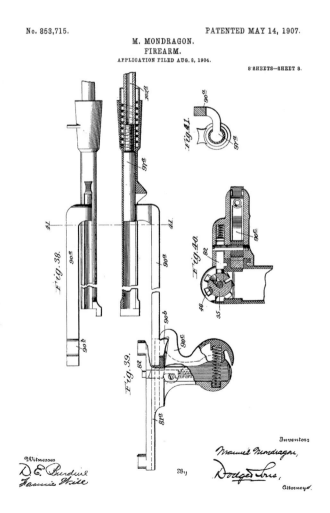

A diagram from the 1907 US patent document filed by Manuel Mondragón for his self-loading rifle. The document shows parts of the bolt group and the gas-operated mechanism. (US Gov)

The Kar 98k was a 7.92×57mm Mauser rifle. Although accurate and robust, its tactical application was limited by its integral box magazine, which held just five rounds, and its bolt-action mechanism. In capable hands, it could fire about 15 rounds per minute. (Armémuseum; The Swedish Army Museum)

This was far from a dead end – the M1 Garand and myriad other semi-auto rifles would prove that – but such guns were not entirely compatible with the desired full-auto capability, and still gave the shooter's shoulder a good thump with every round discharged. For these reasons, another avenue of investment lay in creating a new cartridge with more controllable recoil, around which automatic rifles could be designed. The principal companies involved in this activity during the first half of the 1930s were Gustav Genschow und Company (Geco), Rheinish-Westphaelische Sprengstoff AG (RWS), Rheinmetall and Deutsche Waffen- und Munitionsfabriken (DWM). By the mid-1930s, various cartridges had emerged, all with reduced case length, including 8×46mm, 7×46mm, 7×39.1mm and 7.75×39.5mm. The latter, developed by Geco, seems to have acquired at least some form of official sponsorship by the Heereswaffenamt (Army Ordnance Office), and a weapon was designed to take the round.

The Vollmer M35 automatic carbine was the creation of one Heinrich Vollmer, and it ran along the lines of an earlier Vollmer self-loading design, the 7.92×57mm Selbstladegewehr 29 (SG 29), a design earlier rejected by the Heereswaffenamt. At this time, the German ordnance authorities were still somewhat suspicious – for no sound reason – of gas-operated weapons that tapped propellant gas directly off the barrel. Vollmer's gun used a different form of gas mechanism, similar to the Bang system described earlier, with a gas-powered muzzle nozzle unlocking the bolt and pushing it through its recoil phase.

There seems to have been considerable promise in the Vollmer system. During early firing trials at Biberach in June 1935, it demonstrated the ability to eat through the contents of 20-round detachable box magazines at a rate of 1,000rpm, although the high ammunition consumption did not endear it to the authorities. Revised and improved models were produced later in the year, curing feed and ejection problems. In its A35/II version, the Vollmer rifle gave impressive performance during further trials in 1937, especially in terms of its reliability. Following rate-of-fire reductions to 300–400rpm, by early 1938 the Heereswaffenamt seemed

to be considering adopting the rifle as an official weapon of the Heer. Testing continued to produce glowing results with the updated A35/II, but then in August 1938 the interest from the Heereswaffenamt stopped dead, with little explanation.

The Vollmer was essentially history's first automatic rifle to fire an intermediate cartridge, and why development ceased is puzzling. Automatic rifles are certainly more complicated and expensive to produce than bolt-action counterparts, and war-production considerations might have been foremost in the minds of the Heereswaffenamt. However, the former director of Geco, H.G. Winter, after the war gave his thoughts on the reason:

The Soviet SVT-38 rifle was partly the inspiration behind the Gew 41 and Gew 43 rifles. It fired the 7.62×54mmR cartridge from a ten-round detachable box magazine. (Armémuseum; The Swedish Army Museum)

> The weapons developed by Vollmer in the years 1935–39 were excellent, and were especially attractive through their reliability, as was the ammunition. However, the responsible military departments at the time, by and large, did not recognize the uniqueness of this new type of weapon and ammunition, to have encouraged and recommended its further development by all means possible. Only General Kittel, who at that time still only held the rank of Major, had realized its importance. (Quoted in Senich 1987: 49)

From one perspective, Winter's explanation certainly seems plausible. The combination of bolt-action rifle, submachine gun and machine gun that armed the Heer probably didn't seem to have pressing problems when it came to killing people on the battlefield. Furthermore, the Germans had not yet encountered the combat advantages possessed by an opponent armed with a semi-automatic rifle; fighting against the Soviets from 1941 and the Americans from 1942 would remove this veil from German eyes.

Looking from another angle, however, we see that even as the Vollmer weapon was fading from the scene, the German ordnance authorities were still maintaining their commitment to the intermediate-cartridge concept. In fact, the Heereswaffenamt may well have been working against the tide

of opinion flowing from the General Staff; Hitler himself was no proponent of the medium-range rifle concept, and felt that every infantryman should be able to command ranges of up to 1,200m. Nevertheless, the Heereswaffenamt continued to support development of automatic rifles, albeit with a focus on more realistic war-production costs. In 1938 they issued specifications for a new type of rifle to C.G. Haenel Waffen- und Fahrradfabrik, based in Suhl, whose director was the great Hugo Schmeisser.

The specifications issued are revealing, as they show that even in the immediate years before World War II, the concept of what would become the assault rifle was already embedded in military thinking:

- The gun had to demonstrate reliability even in sub-zero or desert conditions.
- It had to be resistant to the ingress of dust and dirt.
- Its operating mechanism had to be simple (this prescription might have been issued with the recent Vollmer weapons in mind).
- It had to weigh no more, and preferably less, than the standard German Army bolt-action rifle, the Kar 98k (3.9kg).
- Its overall length had to be shorter than the Kar 98k (1,110mm).
- The gun should offer the option for full-auto fire at a controllable level of recoil and rate of fire (350–400rpm was suggested).
- Semi-auto fire needed to be accurate out to 400m.
- Full-auto bursts were to be effective out to 400m.
- It needed to have the option for fitting a grenade-launching attachment.

Here the demand was for a rifle that was shorter and lighter than the standard infantry rifle, but which could handle semi- and full-auto fire over realistic combat ranges. This aspiration still required an effective cartridge to go with it, so the Polte-Werke company in Magdeburg was given the task of perfecting a cartridge for Haenel's weapon. From early 1940, the great Walther gun manufacturer also managed to involve itself in the race to develop a new automatic rifle. (It received an official contract to continue development in 1941.) Note that the Heereswaffenamt added a further stipulation to the design criteria – the gun had to be simple to manufacture, with as few machining processes as possible and a greater reliance upon stamping and welding.

The story of Haenel's and Walther's efforts to produce a fresh breed of infantry weapon occupies the first three years of the war, the gestation of the new designs prolonged by Germany's immersion in a conflict on multiple fronts. Progress was also hampered by Polte's attempts to perfect an assault cartridge. They finally did so in 1940 with the 7.92×33mm *kurz* (short) round. The cartridge was essentially a shortened version of the 7.92×57mm rifle round, necked down and fitted with a lightened bullet (*c.* 126gr/8.19g). Total case length was 47.6mm, and its muzzle velocity was in the region of 685m/sec, compared to about 820m/sec of the Mauser round. It offered the right blend of range, penetration, weight and recoil required by the new assault rifle.

A striking view of the right-hand side of the MP 43. The aperture over the ejection port is open, showing the hooked bolt-guiding piece at the top. The simple use of metal stamping in the manufacture is evident in the finish of the receiver. (Chuck Norton)

During 1940, Haenel produced two prototype weapons for the *kurz* cartridge. In broad terms, the Maschinenkarabiner 42 (MK 42; Machine Carbine 42) was a gas-operated rifle firing from an open bolt.[1] The initial firing mechanism used a tilting-bolt locking mechanism, in which the gas piston lifted the bolt into a locked position against the breech, or lowered it for unlocking. Feed was via a 30-round magazine, based largely on that used for the MP 38 submachine gun. In overall appearance it was not dissimilar to the later MP 44, with the exception of a more obtrusive gas-piston mechanism extending beneath the barrel. As per the specification, the gun could be set for semi- or full-auto fire, and a threaded muzzle allowed the fitting of a rifle-grenade attachment.

Trials of the MK 42 in 1941–42 went well enough for the Heereswaffenamt to authorize the gun for production, albeit with a good number of modifications to the design, including the switch to a closed-bolt operating system. Haenel began manufacturing the gun as the MKb 42(H) in the winter of 1942/43, but production figure never grew to the intended 10,000 units per month; in total 12,000 of the units were series produced between November 1942 and July 1943. These were small numbers given the scale of the German armed forces, but the MKb 42(H)'s lasting legacy was as the bedrock for the subsequent MP 43 series.

While Haenel was busy with the MKb 42(H), Walther had also been pushing forward to meet the new specification. It had in fact been working on self-loading rifles since 1937, including a gas-operated semi-automatic weapon called the Model A115 No. 3 in 1941, although this fired the standard 7.92×57mm rifle round. Using this basic design, however, plus the Polte cartridge, Walther produced the MKb 42(W). Despite the fact that Walther was more experienced in sheet-metal production techniques than Haenel, it was still playing catch-up with Haenel's development programme, and prototypes of the weapon weren't available until the beginning of 1942.

The MKb 42(W) had much in common with the Haenel competitor, particularly in the nature of the receiver construction and magazine housing.

[1]　In an open-bolt weapon, the bolt is held back under tension until the trigger is pulled, at which point the bolt, under pressure from the return spring, feeds, chambers and fires a cartridge in one action. The shift in mass results in a less accurate weapon than a closed-bolt gun, i.e. one in which the bolt is forward and locked prior to pulling the trigger, when only the firing pin moves. The advantage of open-bolt guns, however, is that they control heat build-up better during full-auto firing.

It was a gas-operated weapon firing from a closed bolt and fed from 30-round magazines. One sophisticated feature was a last-round bolt hold-open device; this held the bolt back in the open position when the last round of the magazine had been fired, alerting the soldier to the empty magazine and helping cool the weapon after bursts of fire. The Walther's firing mechanism was of high quality, featuring double torsion springs, and elements of this mechanism would later be found in the MP 43 (although whether these features had also been developed separately by Haenel is a subject of ongoing debate). What was equally significant about both weapons was that they exhibited the 'straight-in-line' design layout demonstrated by many modern assault rifles. By placing the barrel, receiver, bolt-mechanism and stock in a clean horizontal line straight back into the user's shoulder, the guns were controllable to fire, even on full-auto.

An MP 43 stripped down to its major component parts. Note how the pistol-grip unit hinges downwards to provide easy access to the trigger group for cleaning. The gas piston and bolt carrier are in the middle left of the picture. (Chuck Norton)

One interesting aside to the development of the MKb 42(H) and MKb 42(W) is that both were adapted for fitting telescopic sights, specifically the 1.5× Zielfernrohr, to extend their effective combat range out to 600m. The practical outcome of this plan is unclear, as is the thinking behind it, given the inherent limitations of the cartridge. Certainly, the scepticism towards the assault rifle concept from Hitler and others might have prompted the Heereswaffenamt to develop ways to extend the range capability of the weapons, and hence stray into the territory of bolt-action rifles.

Both the MKb 42(H) and MKb 42(W) would have a troubled journey through the Wehrmacht's convoluted and mercurial weapons trial process in 1941 and 1942. Various tests were conducted at locations throughout Germany, and by the end of 1942 the upshot was that the MKb 42(W) was essentially out of the race, deemed too complicated for wartime production and too mechanically sensitive for front-line use, while the MKb 42(H) was nearing final approval for production. Yet by now, the Haenel gun was not the only new direction in German small-arms design.

A Waffen-SS soldier is seen here with an MKb 42(H), taking aim from his trench on the Eastern Front. Only about 8,000 of the MKb 42(H) variant were produced, although the design mutated into the MP 43. (BArch, Bild 101III-Hoppe-082-22, Hoppe)

DIFFERENT OPTIONS

During the early years of World War II, the German forces were becoming increasingly aware of the use of semi-automatic rifles in foreign armed forces. The United States had adopted the M1 Garand, a formidable piece of personal firepower. The Soviets were investing in semi-auto technology; having broken ground with the 6.5mm Federov 'Avtomat' back in the pre-Revolution days, they were now advancing matters with the 7.62×54mmR Simonov AVS-36 and the same-calibre Tokarev SVT-38 in the late 1930s. Unlike the intermediate-cartridge developments, these weapons chambered full-power rifle cartridges fed from relatively low-capacity magazines, and firing in semi-auto mode only.

In 1943, a US War Department report acknowledged a new weapon captured by Allied forces in the North African theatre. It was described as follows:

a. General
Recent shipments of captured enemy ordnance equipment from North Africa included two specimens of the new German 7.92-mm (.312 in.) semi-automatic rifle, the G. 41. It is a gas-operated, 10-shot, magazine-fed shoulder weapon weighing 10 lbs. 14 oz. [4.9kg]. The over-all length is 45 inches [1,143mm], the length of the barrel 22 inches [558.8mm]. (US War Dept 1943)

The Gew 41, to give the weapon its full name, was a relatively recent addition to the Wehrmacht arsenal at the time it fell into US hands.

It had emerged from a competitive programme for a new semi-auto rifle, initiated in 1940. Mauser and Walther were the main participants, and had produced prototype weapons with similar layouts and operating mechanisms. Both, for example, utilized a version of Bang's gas mechanism. The US War Department report explained this system in detail in its report:

b. Functioning
It is operated by having the muzzle blast trapped by a cone-shaped muzzle cap and directed against a gas piston in the gas cylinder. The piston is in the form of a collar which fits around the barrel. This piston impinges against a light piston rod which is located over the barrel under a plastic hand guard. The rear of this piston rod contacts the movable locking and unlocking cover on top of the bolt. This cover is connected to the firing-pin housing which is housed within the bolt assembly. As the cover is driven rearward $\frac{9}{16}$ inch by the piston rod, it pulls the firing-pin housing back, causing the two movable locking lugs in the bolt head to be withdrawn from the locking recesses in the receiver by a camming movement. The bolt is then free to move, and residual pressure in the barrel drives the bolt rearward, ejecting the spent round and cocking the mechanism. As the bolt moves to the rear it also actuates the hammer, compressing the hammer spring and causing the hammer notch to be engaged by the sear. After the bolt stops its rearward motion, it returns forward under the impetus of the compressed recoil-springs in the bolt body, strips a new round from the magazine, and inserts it into the chamber. As the bolt closes, the two locking lugs are driven sidewards through holes in the bolt-head into the locking recesses in the receiver walls by the camming action of the firing-pin housing. Positive locking at the moment of firing is ensured by cams cut on the firing-pin housing, which make it necessary for the locking lugs to be clear of the firing-pin housing before the firing pin can contact the primer of the round in the chamber. (US War Dept 1943)

The 7.92×57mm Mauser cartridge delivered a muzzle velocity of 775m/sec from a 546mm barrel, and its range was comparable to that of the Kar 98k. The rifles were actually longer and heavier than the bolt-action weapon, the only advantages offered seeming to be the semi-auto function and the extra five rounds in the magazine when compared to the standard-issue rifle. (The Gew 41 weapons, however, had integral magazines, reloaded via clips inserted through the open bolt.)

Mauser's Gew 41(M) model was not destined for great things. The weapon proved unreliable in trial and combat, and of the 6,673 produced nearly 1,700 were returned to Mauser as mechanically unusable, and Mauser's participation in the programme came to an end. The Walther version – the Gew 41(W) – was manufactured in smaller numbers (up to 7,500 in total), but it was to become the foundation of the standard production model, known straightforwardly as the Gew 41 from December 1942, of which 120,000 were made.

The Gew 41 semi-automatic rifle. This photograph clearly suggests the muzzle-heavy design of the Gew 41, by virtue of the muzzle cup and the actuating mechanism. (Chuck Norton)

A close-up view of the ring-shaped muzzle cone and threaded muzzle of the Gew 41. On firing, propellant gases were trapped in the cone, which in turn deflected the gases backwards to operate an annular piston and operating rod, unlocking and driving the bolt back against the recoil spring. (Chuck Norton)

Walther's incarnation of the Gew 41 was an improvement over the Mauser firearm largely because it had ignored some of the specifications laid down by the German high command. The three key requirements of the framework were:

1. The barrel could not be bored through as part of the gas mechanism.
2. No part on the upper surface was allowed to move with the automatic loading movements.
3. If the automatic mechanism failed, the rifle had to keep going, being capable of manual loading in the manner of the Kar 98k.

It appears that Mauser diligently stuck with every aspect of this specification, whereas Walther ignored the second and third parts, thereby making a simpler rifle than Mauser. 'Simple' was, however, a strictly relative term with the Gew 41, as even in its final form it was an expensive and complicated weapon to produce, as well as being heavy and unreliable in the field. It managed to persist in service until the end of the war, although production stopped in 1943 with the introduction of a more convincing semi-auto rifle, the Gew 43.

The Gew 43 was the product of lessons learned from all that was wrong with the Gew 41, both from a combat perspective and from wartime production requirements. It was also inspired by captured examples of the Soviet SVT-40, which showed that an accurate semi-auto rifle firing full-power cartridges was a viable prospect. Three companies were involved in its manufacture – Walther, Berliner-Lübecker Maschinenfabrik and Gustloff-Werke – although Walther was the first to begin production. Out went the Bang system and in came a conventional gas cylinder and piston arrangement. Other improvements included the introduction of a detachable magazine (still of ten rounds) to facilitate faster reloading, and a more streamlined production processes, including the use of first laminated wood then plastic for the weapon's furniture. Note that in 1944 the Gew 43 was slightly modified (it was shortened by 50mm and its trigger guard was enlarged) to produce the Kar 43, although the weapon was essentially the same.

The Gew 43 was one of the relative success stories in the history of German wartime self-loading weapons. It was made in significant numbers – more than 402,000 – and it saw widespread combat service. Interestingly, some 53,400 examples of the weapon were actually intended purely for

A disassembled Gew 41. The magazine spring and integral magazine can be seen in the centre-left of the picture; the Gew 41 was loaded with two five-round Mauser rifle stripper clips, which could be pushed down into the gun when the bolt was locked in the rear position. (Chuck Norton)

German mountain troops inspect a Soviet AVT-40 semi-automatic rifle on the Eastern Front. The Soviet applications of semi-auto rifles were a significant inspiration behind the development of similar German weapons. (Cody Images)

semi-auto sniping duty, once fitted with the 4× Zielfernrohr 4 (Zf 4) telescopic 'scope. (The applications and relative success of the German semi-auto sniper weapons are assessed in the following chapter.)

Even though the Gew 43 was made in greater numbers than any other semi-auto/auto weapon, it still was unable to change the face of German front-line firepower. By the middle years of the war, the German front-line army numbered in the millions not the thousands, and ultimately bolt-action rifles were quicker to run off lathes and other machines. But even as the course of the war started to turn against Germany, the Third Reich war machine continued to invest time, energy and materials into producing new forms of weaponry. This continued to be the case with the automatic rifles, as Germany's weapons producers inched towards what we now truly identify as the assault rifle.

A fine front view of a Gew 43. Key improvements of the Gew 43 when compared to the Gew 41 were its detachable box magazine, which facilitated faster reloading, and its more conventional and reliable gas-cylinder and piston operating mechanism. (Joseph Magers)

THE FG 42

The Fallschirmjägergewehr 42 (Paratrooper's Rifle 42) – to give it its full name – was designed purposely for the Luftwaffe's airborne forces, which had formed in 1936. By the early campaigns of World War II, the Fallschirmjäger were already regarded as an elite force within the Wehrmacht, demonstrated by operations such as the raid on Eben Emael in May 1940 and the major airborne invasion of Crete in 1941. The latter operation, however, had inflicted near-Pyrrhic losses upon the German paratroopers, and threw a harsh spotlight on the gaps in unit firepower. By the very nature of their deployment, the Fallschirmjäger could only take light weaponry into action; the poor design of their parachutes meant that the paras jumped into action armed only with a pistol and grenades on their person, while other small arms had to be retrieved from separately dropped containers. In the absence of heavier support fire, apart from a few machine guns and light mortars, the suppressive capabilities offered by the Kar 98k rifle and the MP 38/MP 40 submachine guns were limited.

Thus in November 1941 the Luftwaffe's Unterkommission zur Entwicklung von Automatischen Waffen (Sub-committee for the Development of Automatic Arms) issued a requirement for a new automatic weapon for the Fallschirmjäger. It had to offer firepower equivalent to that of a light machine gun, but also be portable enough for it to be carried during a parachute jump, via a special harness, and to be wielded like a rifle. The list of criteria issued by the commission was

LEFT
The rear receiver of the Gew 43. The flip safety switch seen at the very end of the receiver is in its 3 o'clock 'safe' position; to fire the weapon the user had to move the switch over to the 9 o'clock position. (Joseph Magers)

RIGHT
The rear sight of the Gew 43, as seen here, was adjustable for ranges of up to 1,100m, in 100m increments. The maximum practical range of the weapon, however, was more in the region of 600m. (Joseph Magers)

similar in many ways to that given out by the Heereswaffenamt regarding the design of a new army automatic rifle. The gun had to be less than 1m in length, and lighter than the Kar 98k. It required a detachable magazine of at least 20 rounds and a selective-fire facility. It also had to take rifle-grenade adaptors and be fitted with a small bayonet.

There were some distinctive keynotes of the specification, however. The gun had to be practical in terms of firing from the hip, a concession to assault tactics but also to the possibility of a para firing the weapon during a parachute descent. It was to have the option of mounting a 1.5× optical sight, a sophisticated fitment balanced by the more medieval requirement that the gun's shape allow it to be used as a club in hand-to-hand combat. (Because paratroopers are often deployed well beyond the reach of immediate resupply, the possibility of their running out of ammunition is always distinct.) The new weapon was to take the standard 7.92×57mm rifle cartridge; here was a weapon that had to deliver punch. To add to the design challenge, however, the weapon had to offer full-auto fire, so recoil control was going to be something of a challenge.

The commission's requirements for the new weapon must have read like wishful thinking to many weapons designers. Note, for example, the following general description of the weapon's overall layout and tactical use:

The FG 42/I was a ground-breaking design on many levels. Here we see two side profiles of the weapon, plus a close-up of the basic muzzle brake (top right) and a view through the magazine aperture to the bolt group inside. (Claus Espeholt)

It is preferable to construct the weapon in such a way, that it fires from a closed breech in semi-automatic mode to improve accuracy, but after switching to full-automatic from an open breech. Barrel changing is not required. The barrel should have a life expectancy of at least 2000 shots, also if short bursts are sometimes fired. A rifle-

like butt and stock are not required, but normal firing from the shoulder without support must be guaranteed. A second pistol grip for the left hand is preferred. To prevent obstruction during the jump, folding the stock should be possible. For firing from the prone position it has to be fitted with a simple, folding support. The construction of the shoulder stock can be made to assist in absorption of the recoil.

The gun has to function stably in full-automatic fire without jumping. The prevention of fouling from external source is of special importance. Insensitivity to blows and shock, which follow from its use, is extremely important. (Quoted in de Vries 2012: 12)

Given the times and the state of firearms development, the commission's specification was a serious challenge. Yet several companies stepped forward into the development arena, principally Krieghoff, Gustloff, Haenel, Großfuss, Rheinmetall-Borsig and Mauser-Werke. The companies took a variety of different routes up the mountain. The sporting gun manufacturer Krieghoff, for example, selected its Model 1940 aircraft machine gun, adapted its layout for hand-held use and replaced the belt-feed mechanism with magazine feed. Mauser made a similar adaptation of its MG 81 aircraft machine gun. Both designs quickly fell from grace – given the nature of the specification, what was required was a ground-up new design, which the Luftwaffe received courtesy of engineer Louis Stange, working at Rheinmetall's Sömmerda works.

Stange revealed prototypes of his new weapon – initially known as the Gerät 450 – in February and March of 1942, and improved versions emerged for testing during the spring of that year. Demonstrations of the weapon to the Luftwaffe's top brass were enthusiastically received (by this time the Gerät 450 was the only horse in the race for the new Fallschirmjäger rifle), and in September 1942 the rifle was finally accepted for production and Luftwaffe adoption, with an initial order for 2,000 rifles by Christmas 1942. It was at this time that the rifle was also given its FG 42 title.

The first model of the FG 42 – the FG 42/I – was strikingly different from any other rifle in service around the world at the time. Made extensively from pressed and stamped components, the rifle had a 'straight-in-line' layout that channelled the recoil of the 7.92×57mm round directly back into the flared stock and the shooter's shoulder. Further recoil management was provided by an internal buffer system, but also a muzzle brake. The all-metal gun featured an acutely slanted pistol grip and a 10- or 20-round box magazine, side-mounted to the left of the receiver. This placement meant that the magazine housing did not dictate the placement of the pistol grip and trigger group, resulting in a shortened weapon just 945mm long yet retaining a useful barrel length of 500mm, delivering a muzzle velocity of 740m/sec. Rate of fire was a crackling 900rpm.

The innovations extended to the FG 42's internal workings. As required by the specification, the gun fired from a closed bolt during semi-auto fire – making it more accurate – and an open bolt in full-auto

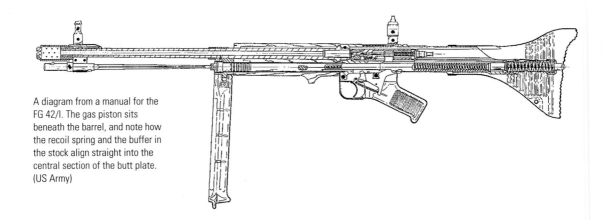

A diagram from a manual for the FG 42/I. The gas piston sits beneath the barrel, and note how the recoil spring and the buffer in the stock align straight into the central section of the butt plate. (US Army)

The FG 42/II was a significant redesign of the original FG 42 weapon, especially in the changed location of the bipod mount. In these images we also see the Zf 4 telescopic sight fitted to some FG 42s, in the expectation of turning them into precision marksman's weapons. (Claus Espeholt)

mode, improving the cooling of the weapon.[2] The FG 42 was a gas-operated weapon, gases being tapped off from the barrel to drive back a gas piston and the attached bolt. Note that the yoke of the gas piston featured the firing pin, which ran through the hollow bolt, and the bolt head had two opposing locking lugs to lock the bolt firmly into place at the moment of firing. Semi- or full-auto fire was selected via a thumb-operated selector switch on the left side of the trigger guard; the cocking handle was on the right side of the receiver. For stable shooting, the FG 42 came with a folding steel bipod, hinged just in front of the short ribbed foregrip. A special clamp allowed fitment of a 4× ZfG 42 telescopic sight (although the GwZf 4 was used on later models), which was set on the top of the receiver just over the rear aperture sight, while just beneath

2 While submachine guns can fire from a closed bolt on full-auto quite comfortably, with the full-power rifle cartridge the heat build-up can result in 'cook off', the involuntary firing cartridges purely from the heat of the chamber.

the muzzle was an integral spike bayonet, which could be swung forward and locked into position.

As we shall see in the following chapter, the FG 42 was not a perfect weapon, but it was a striking glimpse of things to come. The biggest challenge, however, was getting it into production. The wartime demands on Rheinmetall meant that by mid-1943 the FG 42 was still not in production. Furthermore, trials and field testing of pre-production models in the interim had resulted in a whole new raft of required improvements to the design. In the end, it was decided to get Krieghoff to produce the first model of the FG 42. This output began in May/June 1943, but quality and function problems with the initial weapons meant that the Fallschirmjäger actually didn't take them into combat until early 1944.

Thereafter the FG 42 would go through several stages of improvement and modification. The reasons for this continuing evolution are explained in more detail in the following chapter, but an outline of the developments is useful here. In the summer of 1943, the Sömmerda plant began development of another model of the FG 42, although this would prove to be an intermediate step on the way to an authorized second model. The modifications of this gun compared to the original design were extensive, but the most significant were a bipod mount relocated to the muzzle of the gun; a lower rate of fire (750rpm) courtesy of a heavier bolt assembly; the introduction of a gas regulator; a laminated wood stock.

Just 210 of the 'intermediate' model FG 42 were produced, and mainly served as test beds to refine the second production model, which was authorized for manufacture and issue by the Reichsluftfahrtministerium (RLM; Reich Ministry of Aviation) from January 1944. In many respects, the second model was largely the same as the interim model, with subtle changes to various components. The gun was, however, designed to be heavier overall and therefore more robust, and there were some changes to allow for improved ease of production.

Krieghoff was again given the production order, this time for 120,000 guns, although subsequent issues of manufacturing capacity meant that

A Luftwaffe Obergefreiter takes aim and opens fire with an FG 42/I in Italy in 1942/43. This photograph is one of a series of propaganda shots. Note how the bayonet is extended during firing. (BArch, Bild 101I-576-1831-27A, Hanns Groß)

L.O. Dietrich of Altenburg and Wagner & Co. of Mülhausen were later commissioned to help speed things up. A catalogue of disasters and inefficiencies nevertheless meant that the first batch of the second model only began to come out of the factories in November 1944; these were actually part of an early batch intended for field testing, and full-scale production was scheduled for March 1945.

History would prevent the FG 42 from showing its real impact on the battlefield. Production of the second model totalled about 6,224 weapons, far too few to change the nature of German infantry firepower. For all its simplifications, it also remained an expensive alternative to a pressed-steel MP 40 or a simple bolt-action rifle, and by the last months of the war survival was Germany's priority, not experimental 'luxury' weapons. Nevertheless, the FG 42 would see some combat testing, alongside another assault rifle with a design that would go on to change the face of infantry firearms.

MP 43/MP 44/StG 44

Our story now returns to the MKb 42(H), which went into limited production in November 1942. Only some 11,853 were turned out, the low production figure largely due to Hitler's continuing mistrust of the whole intermediate-cartridge concept and to other developments within the assault-rifle field. Despite Hitler's scepticism, the Heereswaffenamt kept development alive in various ways, supporting trials and refinements of the early design concepts. A key moment on the road to the StG 44 was the production of an improved MKb 42(H), known as the MKb 42(H) *aufschießend*, which had a modified stock and handguard, improved sights and a simplified gas piston system, plus it fired from a closed bolt for enhanced accuracy. The MKb 42(H) compared favourably to the other semi-automatic and automatic rifles then in circulation, and the Heereswaffenamt was keen to take the design forward into more substantial production.

An MP 43/1 is tested at the Infanterie-Schule, Döberitz, in 1943. This weapon is fitted with a Zf 4 optical sight, although full-auto fire from the gun tended to knock the sight off zero. (BArch, Bild 146-1979-118-55, o. Ang.)

THE FG 42 EXPOSED

7.92mm Fallschirmjägergewehr 42

1. Flash hider/muzzle brake
2. Front sight
3. Barrel
4. Gas port
5. Chamber
6. Firing pin
7. Rear sight
8. Bolt assembly
9. Buffer assembly
10. Stock
11. Mainspring
12. Pistol grip
13. Sear
14. Trigger
15. Operating rod
16. Front grip
17. Bipod assembly
18. Gas cylinder
19. Folding bayonet assembly

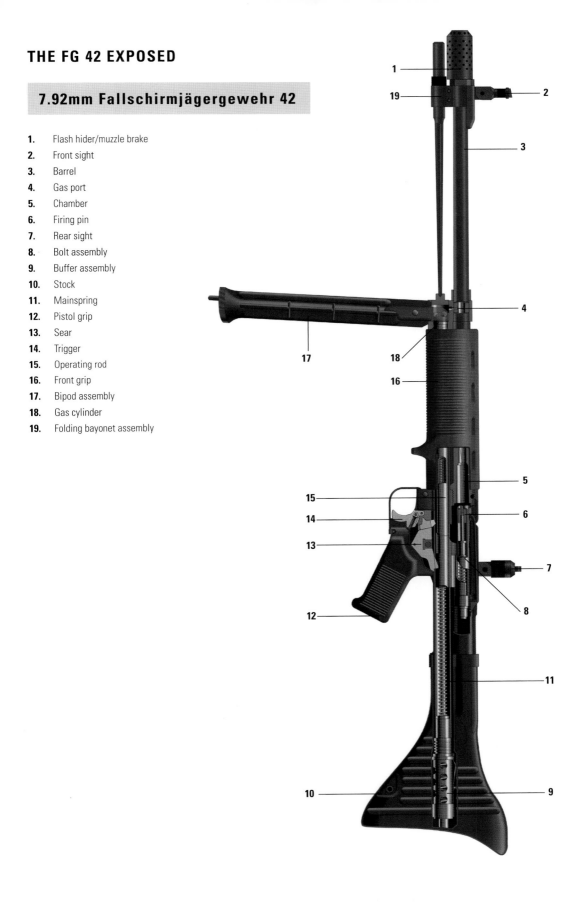

There remained the small problem of Hitler, who had authorized a separate line of selective-fire rifle development by Gustloff-Werke in Suhl. The three Gustloff models that emerged in late 1942, however, all fired the standard 7.92×57mm cartridge. Of the three rifles tested, the Gustloff 206 became the frontrunner, but production would not be able to begin until late 1943 or early 1944. Meanwhile, infantry trials in December confirmed the superiority of the new MKb 42(H) over existing standard-issue small arms, and it also received a new title – Maschinenpistole 43 (MP 43). Tantalizingly, the MP 43 could actually be ready for production by mid-1943, but once again Hitler rejected the weapon following demonstrations in February, banning its further development. With some courage, the Heereswaffenamt kept the weapon alive and even took it to troop trials in April 1943. By the following September senior Heer figures were even recommending its immediate mass production, to alleviate the problems of German soldiers on the Eastern Front adopting Soviet automatic small arms to boost their squad firepower.

A German infantryman on the Eastern Front trudges through the mud carrying his MP 43/1. Conditions on this front tested the Sturmgewehr's reliability to the utmost; if it was kept clean and properly oiled, it tended to function reliably. (Cody Images)

The issue of Hitler's approval for the weapon could no longer be avoided. His position was eventually shifted by Karl-Otto Saur, the chief of the technical department to the Reichsministerium für Bewaffnung und Munition (Reich Minister of Armaments and War Production) Albert Speer, who used the persuasion provided by positive field evaluations to change Hitler's mind. Thus Hitler ordered the MP 43 into production, with a view to its replacing the MP 38 and MP 40 submachine guns. The Army even had grandiose visions of its replacing the Kar 98k, in a similar way to how the M1 Garand had replaced the M1903 Springfield in the US Army.

A weary-looking German soldier carries his MP 44 slung around his neck. The Sturmgewehr was significantly heavier than the standard Kar 98k rifle – 5.1kg as opposed to 3.9kg. (Claus Espeholt)

Yet these were the middle years of World War II, and the hard realities of total war were beginning to bite into the German war economy. Ambitious production totals of some 100,000 MP 43s per month, set in January 1944 by Speer, were in fact totally unrealizable in the context of a Reich sliding towards defeat. Furthermore, it soon became clear that supplies of the new ammunition type would also fall well behind front-line demands.

Nevertheless, the weapon's adoption was not in question, and following further trials by the German 1. and 32. Infanterie-Divisionen the MP 43 was ordered for issue to specific units on 25 April 1944. The MP 43 was also redesignated at this time as the MP 44. The MP 43/MP 44 had been going through various subtle modifications and updates during its early years of development. The MP 43/1, for example, was adapted so that it could take the Gewehrgranatgerät 42 grenade launcher fitting. Yet to all intents and purposes, the MP 44 was essentially the MP 43. A further, and final, change in nomenclature came in December 1944. Hitler, with his growing affection for giving weapons fearsome names, relabelled the MP 44 as the Sturmgewehr 44 (Assault Rifle 44). Although there were some minor tweaks in terms of finish and materials, the design of the weapon remained largely the same.

The StG 44 was a truly impressive firearm for its day. With an overall length of just 940mm, and an empty weight of 5.1kg, it was a portable and convenient weapon to handle, although the receiver often appears to be quite a deep handful when the gun is seen being carried by individuals of shorter stature. It could fire its 30-round magazine at a rate of 500rpm, far exceeding anything that the Allies could field, at least on the scale of a hand-held rifle. As we shall see in the next chapter, although the MP 43 series of weapons couldn't to any degree change the outcome of the fighting in World War II, they could make other armies sit up and think about the future of small arms and small-arms ammunition.

Before moving on to look at the applications of the above weapons on the field of battle, there is one more weapon that needs a brief inclusion. The creation of the last-ditch Volkssturm forces in October 1944 generated an additional need for weaponry. The Volkssturm were recipients of anything the Heer or Waffen-SS could dispense with, plus large quantities of innovative weaponry such as the Panzerfaust shoulder-launched

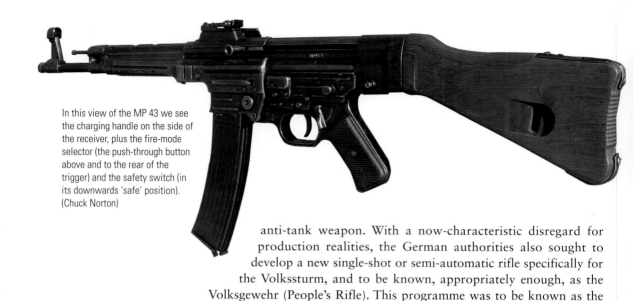

In this view of the MP 43 we see the charging handle on the side of the receiver, plus the fire-mode selector (the push-through button above and to the rear of the trigger) and the safety switch (in its downwards 'safe' position). (Chuck Norton)

Side views of the StG 44. The prominence of the curved 30-round magazine is very evident here; the length and positioning of this magazine made firing from the prone position physically awkward. (Armémuseum; The Swedish Army Museum)

anti-tank weapon. With a now-characteristic disregard for production realities, the German authorities also sought to develop a new single-shot or semi-automatic rifle specifically for the Volkssturm, and to be known, appropriately enough, as the Volksgewehr (People's Rifle). This programme was to be known as the Primitiv-Waffen-Programm (Primitive Weapons Programme), the title giving a full sense of the exigency of the situation.

Despite the late stage of the war, numerous different German arms manufacturers actually attempted to develop the weapon, although Hitler quickly rejected all the single-shot versions in favour of magazine rifles firing the *Kurzpatrone* (short cartridge). One of the frontrunners was the Gustloff VG 1-5, a boxy-looking semi-automatic rifle. On every

A close-up view of the MP 43's bolt-guiding piece, the charging handle projecting from the side. The recoil spring sits above. (Chuck Norton)

level, the VG 1-5 was a tribute to emergency manufacturing processes, it being made from various accumulations of steel tubing, welding and pressed-steel parts. It was notable, however, for its use of a delayed-blowback operating system. A reciprocating hollow sleeve was fitted around the barrel, the sleeve also operating the gun's bolt. When the gun was fired, gas vented through gas ports 65mm from the muzzle and pushed against the sleeve, holding it forward until the pressure had dropped to safe levels, at which point the bolt would open and the gun would reload. The principle was promising, and upwards of 10,000 VG 1-5s were manufactured. Yet the gun also had problems that the wartime situation did not allow time to resolve. It was prone to jamming from fouling, and when the gun became hot barrel expansion could jam the reciprocating sleeve. It stands as one among many acts of futile German inventiveness in the final months of the war.

Our journey through the development of Germany's semi-auto and full-auto rifles has been one of genuine innovation, and as we shall see, the designs that were pioneered would go on to influence many postwar weapons. Now, however, we will look at how Germany's step into self-loading rifles expressed itself in the hands of the front-line soldier.

USE
Technology in combat

A key problem bedevilling historians of Germany's automatic rifles is the relative paucity of front-line combat information that has survived. Although the number of such weapons produced in total was not insignificant, it still pales in comparison with the vast arsenals of standard-issue Wehrmacht small arms. Furthermore, problems with ammunition supply and logistics meant that appreciable numbers of the rifles never actually found their way into soldiers' hands, and remained on racks in German factories. Production itself was critically hampered later in the war by Allied strategic bombing, which ranged far and wide and demolished or damaged many arms-production facilities.

Much of the documentation used to study historical small-arms performance can be incidental – the general first-hand accounts and after-action reports that unwittingly reveal critical details. These are unfortunately thin on the ground for the weapons studied here, but they are not completely absent. Enough remains of either German or Allied responses to and reflections on the weapons to piece together a solid impression of how the guns actually performed in the field. Furthermore, performance comparisons between different contemporary guns can further elucidate our understanding of these weapons.

The first of the new rifles to enter German service were the Gew 41 and Gew 43. The Gew 41's performance on the Eastern Front – where it was principally issued – was not auspicious. As an assault weapon it failed on several counts. First, the Bang-type operating system created a weapon that was very muzzle-heavy, meaning that in a close-quarters situation it was awkward to manoeuvre; at least the Kar 98k was relatively well balanced. Furthermore, the ten-round magazine may have been an improvement over the capacity of the Mauser, but by being an integral rather than detachable magazine (it was loaded through the open bolt with two five-round Mauser clips) it didn't have the quick-reload facility that should support any automatic weapon.

The Gew 41 also had its fair share of reliability problems, particularly once exposed to the mud and freezing weather of the Eastern Front, or the invasive dust of the North African theatre. The muzzle-trap system proved to be especially vulnerable to all these climatic conditions, but the gun was also internally prone to failure from carbon fouling. The corrosive effects of primer compounds on the operating mechanism, leading to further jamming, added to a general lack of confidence in the weapon.

The Gew 43, issued to front-line troops from late 1943, was a better prospect, though still not a perfect one. The extractor was a weak feature of the weapon, and was prone to breaking, and the working parts of the weapon suffered from the wear and tear inflicted by the full-power rifle round. This issue was compounded by the fact that the build quality of the rifles was rather haphazard during the last years of the war, resulting in weapons that frequently failed the tests of resilience while being used in some snow-filled trench on the Eastern Front, or on a sodden mountainside in Italy. (For such reasons, modern weapons collectors are advised against firing vintage Gew 43s, unless they have been substantially checked and improved by a qualified gunsmith.)

Another challenge for the Gew 43 was to find its niche in the firepower spectrum of German forces. By firing the full-power cartridge from a semi-automatic mechanism, the Gew 43 was unsuited to the long-range sniping handled by the Mauser bolt-action rifles. Conversely, at close ranges the infantry's submachine guns were often the more practical option. Yet fitted with a telescopic sight, the Gew 43 found a role as what would today be classified a 'marksman' rifle, delivering accurate fire against individual targets over ranges of up to 600m. Moreover, on the Eastern Front the Red Army's volume assault tactics – essentially human waves – meant that the combination of mid-range accuracy and rapid fire was useful. Here Eastern Front veteran Sepp Allerberger remembers the grim efficiency of the weapon when countering a Soviet attack:

Apparently unnoticed I had thrown myself down some distance from the two wounded Germans remaining in the open, playing dead and hoping to gain for myself the element of surprise. I watched the first two waves of Soviets leave their dugouts, then arose zombie-like from the dead and began firing round after round of accurate fire over open sights at a range of about 80 meters. To be sure of the hit, and for the explosive round to do its work, I aimed for the area just above the hip. With devastating effect each bullet found its mark inside a Russian stomach, destroying a range of inner organs and intestines. The Soviets appeared stunned by having an unexpected apparition firing at them from an oblique angle on the flank, and then became visibly annoyed. Thing were not going to plan for them. In the meantime my ten comrades had gathered their wits and were pouring towards the Russians a blistering fire. The magazine of my semi-automatic held ten

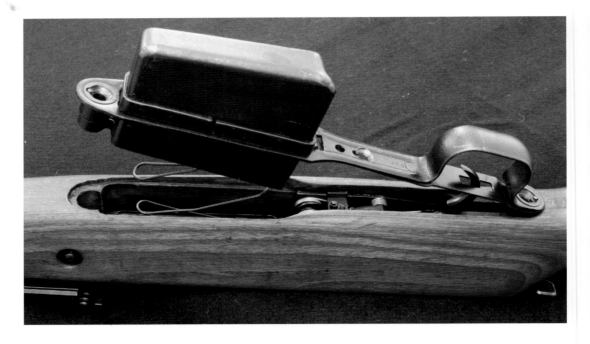

Here we see the integral magazine of the Gew 41 loosened from the stock, the magazine spring clearly visible. Although the Gew 41 only took ten rounds in its magazine, this was still five more than the Kar 98k. (Chuck Norton)

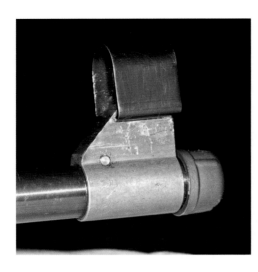

The muzzle of the Gew 43, showing its hooded front sight. The muzzle velocity for the Gew 43 was 746m/sec, almost exactly that of the Kar 98k bolt-action rifle. (Joseph Magers)

rounds. Once the first clip was empty, every shot a hit, I swiftly fitted the second and continued firing. I could see the ground strewn with twenty or more Russian dead or writhing in terrible agony. After reloading with the third clip I became the target of a few desultory replies, but the awful screams of their wounded comrades had unsettled them so much that they aborted the attack and, apart from some withering fire in my direction, retired to their trench. (Wacker 2005)

The advantages of the semi-automatic mechanism plus the ten-round magazine are evident here. This combination enabled Allerberger to switch rapidly between targets without the physical disruption of operating a bolt mechanism, while the mount of the Zf 4 sight, on the right-hand side of the receiver, allowed him to switch between iron sights for close-range work and the telescopic sight for more distant targets.

A notable, and unsettling, element of this account involves the use of explosive ammunition on the Soviet troops. Typically, German snipers were issued with standard *Spitzgeschoss mit Eisenkern* (pointed bullet with iron core; SmE) rifle cartridges, although more astute sharpshooters would attempt to get hold of the best production batches. (Typically these batches consist of ammunition produced at the beginning of a manufacturing run, before minor imperfections are introduced as the production machinery becomes increasingly worn.) Some fortunate snipers managed to obtain the *schweres Spitzgeschoss* (heavy pointed bullet; sS) 7.92mm ball ammunition, this being a high-quality marksman version of the standard rifle cartridge, used in World War I and produced in small (i.e. insufficient) quantities from 1941. Some more ruthless individuals, however, obtained the *Beobachtung-Patrone* (observation cartridge; B-Patrone) exploding round, identified by a black band around the lower half of the bullet. The B-Patrone had been available since the early years of the war, primarily for use by the Luftwaffe (the bright flash emitted by the round on impact was useful for visually correcting fire), but exploding rounds had been banned in an anti-personnel context by the Geneva Convention. Hitler himself – having witnessed the awful effects of such munitions during World War I – was broadly in favour of the ban. The brutal war on the Eastern Front, however, began to shift the goalposts somewhat. Soviet snipers had no qualms about using explosive bullets, and the B-Patrone gradually drifted into unofficial use in 1942 and 1943. In 1944, the bullet was given official sanction, albeit only on the Eastern Front.

A soldier squints through a Zf 41 'scope. Many of the optical sights fitted to German bolt-action and semi-auto rifles were of relatively low power, and served to increase the rifle's effective range to around 600m. (BArch, Bild 101I-279-0923-04, Johannes Bergmann)

As is evident in the account above, the visceral effect of the B-Patrone on the human frame was ghastly in the extreme. Allerberger's tactic of shooting his victims in the abdomen was not unique to him. Sniper historian Martin Pegler notes how German sniper Franz Kramer adopted a similar policy with the Gew 43, as much for inflicting psychological disturbance as physical injury:

> He swapped his K98k for a Model 43 with telescopic sight. He also took four separate magazines filled with B-cartridges [explosive] and put more in his pockets. As the Russians jumped up from their positions and attacked, he suddenly stood up and shot at a distance of 50 to 80 metres in his well-proven method, always at the last wave. With appalling effect his bullets tore into the Russians' torsos, tearing them apart. Every shot was a hit. The Soviets were utterly surprised at this flanking fire ... the attack faltered. After ten shots the magazine was empty, and Franz inserted a fresh one. The screams of the injured were unnerving the others, and they aborted the attack and withdrew. (Pegler 2006: 195)

Note that like Allerberger, Kramer made a conscious swap of his bolt-action rifle for the semi-auto Gew 43. This suggests that those issued with the Gew 43 might have used the semi-auto weapon alongside a Kar 98k or Gew 98, to give themselves tactical flexibility suited to the challenges facing them. Those snipers who opted to use the B-Patrone ammunition would have had to alter the zero of the rifle before doing so, the explosive round having different ballistic properties compared to the standard ball cartridge.

In the Italian theatre and Western Europe following D-Day, the Western Allies also began to encounter the German semi-automatic rifles, with varying responses. For British snipers such as Sergeant Harry Furness, encounters with the Gew 43 often came as part of his counter-sniper role. Here he recounts hunting for a German sniper in France who had already inflicted serious casualties on British troops:

> ... over a long time no further shots were fired, I continued to search for signs using my more powerful scout telescope, and one house I watched for a while ... had broken windows and damaged exterior wooden shutters ... but now and again one of the shutters moved as the wind caught it. I must have been watching the area and that swaying shutter for hours when I caught a little movement – quick movements of any kind draw your eye to it if you are looking. I switched from my telescope to pick up my rifle and it seemed to me to be a hand reaching to get hold of the shutter by the edge. I fired immediately into and near the edge of the shutter, and even without the rifle recoil I felt sure I had seen an arm inside the house slide down and bang on the sill. I waited and watched until dusk before I left but saw no more movement nor had any shot been fired all the time I was there. That night a fighting patrol was sent out and they brought back for me a semi-automatic G43 rifle with a telescopic sight. On the floor next to the window was a dead German. (Quoted in Pegler 2006: 250–51)

Furness does not give his personal impressions of the Gew 43 here, although doubtless the rifle was passed among many hands for careful study. In the following account, US combat armourer Russell E. Spooner tells of examining captured Gew 43s:

> The Fourth Infantry was in position ... and we were here to supply them with replacements. I began to receive many battlefield recoveries, picked up in the local area. Most of them were M1 rifles, with some carbines, and a pair of German Gewehr 43 semi-automatic rifles with the stocks broken and the magazines missing. These were the first examples of a relatively new weapon that I'd seen.
>
> It was interesting that the Germans, who excelled in the design and manufacture of weapons, had been unable to come up with anything to compare with our M1 rifle. Their Gewehr 41 had been a miserable failure... They continually fouled with burnt powder particles and then jammed.
>
> This Gewehr 43 now in my hands was supposed to have overcome that problem and be a weapon superior to our M1. It wasn't, and never would be. It was poorly and cheaply made, with stamped metal parts and casting where machined steel should have been used. It was a prime example of how German ingenuity and manufacturing skill had been undermined by the lack of good materials with which to produce their latest weapons.
>
> The German soldiers who had used these two weapons undoubtedly believed that they had the finest pieces in the world. When Fourth

Infantry riflemen pinned them down in a shell hole, they returned fire until their ammunition ran out. Then they threw their 10-round magazines as far away as they could, smashed the butts of their rifles on the ground to break the stocks, and surrendered. No one, they determined, would be able to use these wonderful weapons against them. No one wanted to, as long as the M1 was available. (Spooner 2005: 230)

Spooner is unstinting here in his criticism of the Gew 43. Much of it is fair, particularly regarding the poor quality of production. On balance, the Garand to which he compares the Gew 43 was indeed superior, a combat-proven piece that gave US soldiers a definite fire superiority in many infantry battles. Yet had the Gew 43's quality issues been resolved, the comparison between the two weapons is perhaps more nuanced. As the data table below illustrates, there was little between the two weapons in terms of overall dimensions and weight. The Garand nevertheless has a significantly longer barrel, which when combined with the powerful .30-06 round gave a superior muzzle velocity. The actual effective ranges of the two weapons were largely equivalent, being comfortably over 400m with iron sights, and ranging beyond 600m with telescopic sights fitted. Yet the Garand was never a very receptive host for telescopic sights. The gun was clip-loaded straight down into the internal magazine via an open bolt, meaning that a telescopic sight could not sit directly over the rear of the receiver. Similarly, the Garand's ejection was performed much further back along the receiver than the Gew 43, a side-effect of the M1's longer

Fallschirmjäger in Belgium in 1944 carry a variety of infantry weapons, including Gew 43 semi-automatic rifles. In a strange deviation from normal issue weapons, however, the man on the left has acquired a British 9mm Sten Gun. (Cody Images)

barrel, whereas the Gew 43 ejected comfortably in front of the Zf 4's front
lens. The sniper variants of the M1 (the M1C and M1D), therefore, had
to be fitted with telescopic sights offset rather awkwardly to the left-hand
side of the gun.

By contrast, every version of the Gew 43 came with a dedicated
sniper rail fitting on the right-rear of the receiver, which allowed for
central fitting of the 'scope. Moreover, by being a standard-issue feature,
the 'scope mount meant that every Gew 43 was capable of being adapted
in an instant for sniper work, rather than this function only being
available on certain dedicated sniper models. The Gew 43 also comes
out well in terms of its loading action. Although the M1 Garand could
be loaded with eight-round clips with some fluidity, the detachable box
magazine system of the Gew 43 was arguably more convenient, and
gave the additional advantage of two extra rounds over the Garand.
Each soldier armed with the Gew 43 usually wore (on the left hip) a
two-pocket set of *Selbstladewaffe-Magazintaschen* (self-loading weapon
magazine pouches), and each pocket could hold a ten-round magazine.
Such was the versatility of the Gew 43 that an empty magazine in situ
could be topped up with the five-round Mauser rifle stripper clips,
pushed in through the opened bolt.

Comparative specifications – Gew 43 and M1 Garand

Data	Gew 43	M1 Garand
Calibre	7.92×57mm Mauser	.30-06
Length overall	1,117mm	1,103mm
Empty weight	4.33kg	4.37kg
Barrel length	558mm	610mm
Magazine	Ten-round detachable box	Eight-round internal box
Muzzle velocity	746m/sec	853m/sec

Side views of the Gew 41(M).
Note the large bolt handle at the
end of the receiver; this was lifted
and pulled backwards to open the
bolt for loading the rifle with
stripper clips. (Armémuseum;
The Swedish Army Museum)

Taking the broad overview, the Gew 43 was potentially the superior when compared to the M1 Garand, had all been well with its production standards. This argument is admittedly artificial, as production quality is integral to the value of a weapon. Nothing turns a soldier against a firearm as much as problems with reliability, and the M1 Garand was noted for its robust resilience to everything the battlefield could throw at it. Had the Gew 43 come earlier in the war, and had chance to go through another couple of phases of improvement, it might well have been one of the conflict's exceptional firearms. The other factor mitigating against the Gew 43 was the simple equation of distribution. Some 400,000 Gew 43s were issued by the end of World War II (about a fifth with telescopic sights), at which point there were more than 4 million M1 Garands in circulation; on the Eastern Front the Soviets manufactured 5.7 million SVT-38/40s between the late 1930s and the end of the war. Thus while the semi-automatic rifle was a ubiquitous or extremely common weapon in some Allied forces, in the German Army those units that did receive the Gew 43 usually limited distribution to one per rifle squad (about 9–13 men).

THE FG 42 IN ACTION

We must be careful not to be seduced by the FG 42. There is much that is patently innovative about the weapon, not least in terms of layout and role, yet it was far from a perfect design. Its limitations were both mechanical and, in a way, tactical also, the core of the problems lying around the choice of cartridge – the 7.92×57mm Mauser.

It is clear that the Allies took special notice of the FG 42 when it first came to their attention in 1944. The US War Department issued the following assessment in their *Intelligence Bulletin* in June 1944:

The Germans have a new 7.92-mm automatic rifle, the F.G. 42 (Fallschirmjäger Gewehr 42), which is a light and versatile weapon, especially suitable for use by German airborne personnel. It should be remembered that the 9-mm machine carbines (M.P. 38/40), which are now in general use, were originally introduced as parachutists' weapons; in like manner, the Germans may well put this new 7.92-mm rifle to more general use in the future.

The new rifle (see figure), which represents a departure in small-arms design, is a close-combat weapon firing any 7.92-mm Mauser rifle ammunition, and combines a relatively light weight with a reasonable degree of accuracy both in single-round and automatic fire. The Germans have struck a balance between the weight limitations of the machine carbine and the power and pressure requirements of the rifle or light machine gun. (US War Dept 1944b)

The quotation accurately sums up the virtues of the FG 42, and notes its 'versatility' as a weapon that could straddle the demands of a submachine gun (machine carbine), rifle and even light machine gun. It also dwells upon the gun's accuracy, a virtue of its 'straight-in-line' design that channelled the force of recoil on a direct line through the stock and into the soldier's shoulder. Given the qualities of the firearm, the report's author envisages the possibility of the FG 42 entering general service.

The Germans who developed and tested the FG 42 were no less impressed by its qualities. After testing the trials version of the weapon in 1943, ordnance officials issued a fairly glowing assessment of its future, once certain 'modifications' were put in place:

The extensive firing trials indicated the necessity of modifications to strengthen several parts and to improve the operational reliability, also under adverse conditions. After the implementation of the modifications it can be anticipated that the FG 42 will operate without malfunctions under all conditions (dirt, cold, heat) up to 10. to 20.000 rounds. The accuracy is equivalent to that of the 98 rifle, as is the ease of handling in all firing positions. When firing from the bipod the middle support offers more advantages; the better ease of handling, as compared to the only slightly better precision with the forward bipod position, is more important in the opinion of the testing facility. The improved version of the telescopic sight can be used even with rough handling and actually simplifies the target acquisition. Compared with the aperture sight, a better hit rate was not recorded. The use of the grenade launcher is possible without alterations. (Quoted in de Vries 2012: 30)

The vision of the FG 42 here is for a near-perfect weapon. It would offer great reliability and 'ease of handling', despite firing a round that was of the same power as the Kar 98k rifle. The location of the bipod (at the front of the gas piston rather than just beneath the muzzle) was deemed a positive advantage from a handling point of view – it would allow a wide degree of traverse to be applied with minimal shoulder movement. Furthermore, its accuracy was excellent, particularly if the gun was married with an optical sight.

A raft of minor and metallurgical modifications went into the first production model of the FG 42. (Note that there were numerous sub-models of the FG 42, each featuring minor variations. The Germans referred to them all as FG 42, however, and here we focus on the three

A famous photograph of one of the Fallschirmjäger involved in the Gran Sasso raid in 1943. He carries one of the early models of the FG 42, which were intended to provide heavier firepower than the rifles and submachine guns available to the rest of the troops. (BArch, Bild 101I-567-1503A-01, Toni Schneiders)

classic divisions of the weapon – first production model, intermediate model, second production model.) The RLM authorized a production batch of 2,000 guns in May 1943, the fulfilment of this order going to Krieghoff. However, the inertia imposed by the conditions of the mid-war years meant that FG 42s did not start rolling off production lines until October 1943, and they were not issued to front-line Fallschirmjäger units until the beginning of 1944. Pre-production models are nevertheless seen in combat photos from mid-1943, exclusively in the hands of paratroopers fighting during the Sicilian and Italian campaigns. The principles on which the early FG 42s were issued are difficult to discern from the photographic evidence. Two unit photographs taken in southern Italy in 1943 show a group of about 30 Fallschirmjäger preparing to go into action. Most are armed with the standard infantry weapons of the Wehrmacht, but one individual is carrying an FG 42 and ammunition bandolier. Other photographs show a similarly limited distribution; when first issued the FG 42 was a long way from being a standard unit weapon.

One of the most famous early appearances of the FG 42 in combat was during the rescue of the Italian dictator Benito Mussolini from the Gran Sasso massif in the Apennine Mountains in September 1943. Mussolini had been deposed and replaced by Marshal Badoglio on 25 July 1943. A German rescue attempt was mounted by a combined force of 2. Fallschirmjägerdivision, Fallschirmjäger-Regiment 7 and 502. SS-Jäger-Bataillon, led by

Major Otto-Harald Mors (the role of the SS officer Otto Skorzeny in leading the action was less influential than history has often claimed). The force was deployed by nine DFS 230 gliders, and freed Mussolini from his army guards without a shot being fired.

The various propaganda photos from the raid show several Fallschirmjäger either holding FG 42s, or displaying the characteristic FG 42 ammunition bandoliers. The bandoliers, worn around the soldier's neck, were made from assorted types of cloth, including 'splinter'-camouflage patterns, and had eight compartments, each receiving one 20-round FG 42 magazine. The total of 160 rounds from such bandoliers would have to be consumed with care, as the FG 42's full-auto rate of fire was 900rpm. Most disciplined soldiers would use their weapon in semi-auto mode only, unless there was a requirement for heavy suppressive fire and there was a good supply of extra ammunition.

In fact, suppressive fire was exactly the reason the FG 42 was taken on the Gran Sasso raid, and it says much about the tactical rationale behind the weapon. One of the bloody lessons learned from the invasion of Crete in 1941 was that airborne invaders require immediate support fire resources if they were to increase their survivability. The vanguard of the Mussolini mission would be provided by Oberleutnant Georg Freiherr von Berlepsch's 1. Kompanie of paratroopers (with an attached 4. Kompanie platoon), and it was this company that received most of the dozen or so FG 42s taken on the mission. The thinking was that, in the absence of heavier supporting weapons (apart from MG 34 machine guns, which could be mounted on the front hatch of the DFS 230 glider after landing), the FG 42s would open up with ripples of automatic fire, should the unit meet stiff resistance upon landing. An FG 42-armed unit could indeed deliver impressive combined fire. The weapon had a conceived practical rate of fire (allowing for magazine changes, cocking, controlled bursts etc.) of *c.* 200rpm. This meant that a dozen such weapons on the ground could give 2,400rpm, equivalent to the practical rate of fire of about five or six MG 42 machine guns. (The reality of how much firepower the rifles could generate is discussed below.) Given that the

FG 42 fired the same round as the MG 42, it was clear that the automatic rifles could make a seminal contribution to the mission. (MG 42s were taken on the raid, but they were not as rapid to deploy as the lighter rifles.) MP 40 submachine guns and Kar 98k rifles filled out the rest of the firepower of the mission.

Some of the photographs from the Gran Sasso raid also show the FG 42 fitted with the ZfG 42 telescopic sight. Telescopic sights were not standard on the FG 42. The first production model's 'iron sights' consisted of a cylindrical rear aperture sight and a corresponding front blade. The threaded base of the aperture sight could be turned up or down to adjust the sighted range, and the aperture provided a more precise alternative to the standard V-notch rear-sight arrangement of most German firearms. The downsides of the aperture sight were that target acquisition often wasn't as quick as with the V-notch, and the sight became more difficult to use in low-light conditions when the small aperture tended to merge visually with the surroundings.

This well-known photograph shows a Fallschirmjäger fighting in the ruins of Monte Cassino, Italy, in 1944. His FG 42/I is propped on a box of grenades; soldiers who used the FG 42 often found that solid objects provided better aids to fire control than the integral bipod. (BArch, Bild 101I-578-1926-36A,

The aperture sight was hinged to allow the fitting of a telescopic sight when necessary, which mounted onto special rails cut into the upper parts of the receiver. Made specifically for the FG 42, but distributed in only limited numbers, the ZfG 42 was not the most powerful of 'scopes (it had a 4× magnification), but it provided enhanced accuracy over short and medium ranges, in much the same way as the Sight Unit Small Arms, Trilux (SUSAT) sight on the British Army's modern SA80 rifles. The ZfG 42 was therefore more a tactical marksman 'scope, rather than a sniper 'scope.

Intermediate model

The FG 42/I gave localized service throughout the Italian theatre in 1943, but significant changes were afoot. Weapons trials in Tarnewitz in the spring, plus feedback from front-line combat units, were producing a raft of recommended modifications. Even as the FG 42/I was issued in late 1943, the July 1943 operator's manual contained an addendum that an improved version of the rifle was on its way.

Many of the modifications focused simply on the challenge of making the FG 42 faster and cheaper to produce under wartime conditions. Yet there were also issues with the weapon's practical operation. The intense rate of fire was proving to be something of a problem. Even the straight-in-line design struggled to cope with the recoil of full-power rifle cartridges rattling off at a rate of 900rpm, and full-auto shot dispersal around the target was broad. The problem was made worse by the FG 42/I's weight and its relatively light barrel – overheating quickly became an issue after

burst-firing a couple of magazines. Firearms expert and historian Robert Bruce conducted modern-day experiments with the FG 42/I in the 1990s, and found the shot dispersal effects a real problem that was only partly solved by good shooting practices:

> This dispersion problem is minimized by firing short bursts from the bipod support, but even then we experienced problems. The flimsy sheet steel bipod has no real lock, so it tends to rock backward with the recoil, and even to collapse. This was overcome by concentrating on keeping a steady forward pressure on the gun – but who needs this sort of distraction in the middle of a firefight? Full automatic fire from the kneeling, crouching, and hipshot positions was only marginally effective except at short range. (Bruce 2010: 87)

These useful observations show how the FG 42/I was really most suited to semi-automatic fire, a very useful combat mode (as the M1 Garand demonstrated) but not delivering the true firepower potential intended for the weapon.

The intermediate model, another Louis Stange production, entered production in the summer of 1943 with Rheinmetall-Borsig, but just 210 units were produced for both trials and for limited field issue. The list of modifications was extensive, but included the following significant redesign:

- The cyclical rate of fire was reduced to 750rpm, partly through the slower reciprocation of a heavier bolt.
- The magazine well was provided with a spring-loaded magazine cover, released by pressing the magazine catch to allow a magazine to be loaded. This feature helped prevent the unwanted ingress of dirt into the mechanism.
- The bipod mount was now moved forward to just beneath the muzzle, with the bipod legs folding forward. The repositioning of the bipod made the gun more stable when delivering automatic fire.
- The angle of the handgrip was reduced to a far more conventional

alignment, and the grip now featured riveted-on wooden grip plates.

- The FG 42/I safety/fire selector switch was modified purely for fire selection; the safety catch itself was located on the left of the handgrip assembly.
- The buttstock was changed to a laminated-wood type, and the butt-release catch was placed at the rear on the right-hand side.
- A gas regulator was added at the position of the Type I's bipod mount assembly. This regulator could be adjusted via a slot on the right-hand side, to control the amount of gas used to power the weapon's cycle (the amount of gas used could be increased as the weapon became dirtier, to apply more power).
- The cylindrical cocking handle of the FG 42/I was replaced with a simple hook.

In addition to these external modifications, a variety of internal parts and mechanisms received various tweaks to improve the FG 42's production-friendliness and its reliability in action.

Following the Italian armistice in September 1943, Fallschirmjäger oversee the disarming of Italian troops in Rome. The soldier in the foreground has an FG 42/I over his shoulder, while his comrade is armed with an MP 40 submachine gun. (BArch, Bild 101I-304-0635-28, Funke)

Issue of the interim model was limited by its low production figures, and was completed by the summer of 1944. The destinations of these weapons are unknown. Although some certainly went to Fallschirmjäger on the Western Front, others may have gone to paratroopers fighting in the Italian theatre. But the evolution of the FG 42 was not yet over. Battlefield and trials feedback continued to trickle back to the authorities in Germany, and at the beginning of 1944 the RLM authorized the production of a second model, the FG 42/II. Optimistically, the production volume was set at 120,000 units, plus 12,000 GwZf 4 telescopic sights, with production overseen by Krieghoff (Krieghoff in turn would use a variety of subcontractors). Manufacture was intended to begin in July 1944, but as usual such aspirations were quickly lost in the sometimes farcical conditions of Germany's looming defeat. One initial delay of several weeks was caused when the master design drawings simply disappeared, and when they were discovered they were damaged to such an extent that they had to be redrawn from scratch. This event was only one of a range of calamities, and consequently the first FG 42/IIs did not emerge from the Krieghoff factory until November 1944. Even the first batch of 500 weapons was not part of the full series production run, being intended as pre-production test weapons. By this time the Reich was being squeezed inexorably in a vice between the collapsing Western and Eastern Fronts. Any sophisticated weapon developments were therefore virtual vanity projects, a distraction from the realities of the war. With the capture of German armaments factories over the coming months, manufacturing output was continually curtailed, so that by the end of the war in May 1945, an estimated 6,173 FG 42/IIs had been made, as opposed to the 120,000 originally conceived.

Returning to the design of the FG 42/II, in many ways it was largely the final version of the interim model. That version had, in its late variants, incorporated a new serrated muzzle-brake design, which was retained in the second production model, as was the overall layout and design. By the time the FG 42/II entered production the FG 42 weapon had undergone a notable transformation from its first incarnation. Some comparative specifications are revealing:

FG 42/I and FG 42/II comparative specifications

	FG 42/I	FG 42/II
Overall length	945mm	975mm
Weight (loaded)	5.18kg	6.65kg
Barrel length	500mm	500mm
Feed	20-round detachable box magazine	20-round detachable box magazine
Rate of fire (cyclical)	900rpm	750rpm
Rate of fire (practical)	250rpm	200rpm
Muzzle velocity	740m/sec	740m/sec

As we can see in these figures, the FG 42 grew longer and substantially heavier between the first and second production models, with an appreciable drop in the rate of fire. For practical battlefield purposes, the latter change would have a minimal impact on the soldier actually using the gun in action. The Germans had proven, to some degree, the value of extremely high rates of fire with the MG 42, which could rip through its belt-fed ammunition at a cyclical rate of fire of up to 1,200rpm. Such weapons could deliver enormous volumes of suppressive fire, although we must always make the distinction between practical and cyclical rates of fire. Another US War Department *Intelligence Bulletin* noted of the MG 42:

> Under battle conditions the MG 42 can fire about 22 bursts per minute—that is, about 154 rounds. Under the same conditions, the MG 34 is capable only of about 15 bursts per minute, at a rate of 7 to 10 rounds per burst, totalling about 150 rounds. Thus the MG 42, used as a light machine gun, requires a slightly higher ammunition expenditure. Although the Germans believe that when the weapon is properly employed, the compactness and density of its fire pattern justify the higher expenditure, recent German Army orders have increasingly stressed the need of withholding machine-gun fire until the best possible effect is assured. (US War Dept 1944a)

Even such a fast-firing weapon as the MG 42 has a practical rate of fire running at around 10 per cent of its cyclical rate. If we apply that same principle to the FG 42/II, then we have a practical rpm more in the region of 75 rounds. Pushing the gun towards its conceived practical rate of 200rpm would not only entail blisteringly quick magazine changes (a 20-round magazine would be emptied in less than two seconds), but the risks of barrel overheating would be pronounced. (The MG 42 had a quick-change barrel, whereas the FG 42's barrel was fixed.)

We therefore have to arrive at some form of general judgement about the success of the FG 42 in fulfilling its original objectives. In some senses the purpose of the FG 42 was rendered irrelevant by the changes of fortune for the German Fallschirmjäger. The gun was conceived specifically as an assault weapon for airborne troops, to boost their suppressive firepower during the early, vulnerable stages of a parachute or glider attack. Yet following the invasion of Crete, Hitler decreed that never again would the Fallschirmjäger be used for large-scale aerial operations. He was true to his word. Apart from some minor specialist airborne actions, the Fallschirmjäger largely served as elite infantry for the remainder of the war, and therefore relied principally on the standard weaponry of the Wehrmacht.

The biggest question mark over the design of the FG 42 was whether it attempted too much in a single weapon. The value of a semi-auto infantry rifle was not in question, enabling an infantryman to pick off multiple targets in quick succession, and to win the battle for fire dominance against soldiers armed with bolt-action rifles. As a light machine gun, however, the FG 42's worth is more debatable.

One of the few enlightening first-hand accounts comes from the pen of a US Army Airborne sergeant, who wrote an after-action report following operations to cross the Rhine in 1945. During the attacks, the sergeant's unit faced resistance from a Fallschirmjäger unit:

> ... we waded off the river bank and made our way slowly to a copse of trees abutting the bank, when suddenly, a (what we thought) MG 34 began to pepper our positions. I told the men to take cover, while we tried to pinpoint the position of the gun, but by then had lost three men to the fire. Another string of bullets rattled off from a different position, hitting Lieutenant _____ five or six times, killing him instantly. It was then that I saw the first German raise up and reposition himself, some two hundred yards [183m] over the bank. He was not, in fact, manning a MG 34, but indeed had one of the dreaded FG 42s in his possession. I made to gather my men to find cover, now knowing what we were up against, when a third FG 42 opened up from a wooded area some two hundred and fifty yards [229m] south of our position, hitting five men in the process. Before we could reposition, maneuver, and counter-attack, the Germans had successfully retreated, not being held up by the weight of a larger machine gun. Our squad took eight casualties while only seeing one German. (Quoted in Dugelby & Stevens 1990)

The adjective 'dreaded' is striking here. While we are used to hearing such terms applied to weapons like the MG 42, the same given to an automatic rifle is rare. It is clear that the sergeant appreciates the FG 42 for several reasons. First is the weapon's accuracy – the US unit is being engaged accurately at ranges of around 200m, and losing men with worrying rapidity. The second is, by implication, the volume of fire the unit is coming under, at first attributed to an MG 34 machine gun. The third, and most important, is that this weight of accurate fire is being delivered by a particularly mobile platform, a weapon which gives machine-gun levels of fire for rifle levels of convenience.

A Fallschirmjäger poses for a propaganda photograph with his FG 42 in France, 1944. The front and rear sights are folded down, and the bipod lies flat against the underside of the barrel. (BArch, Bild 101I-720-0344-11, Wolfgang Wennemann)

If anything, this sergeant's account validates the FG 42 as a tactical light machine gun. Care is needed, however. We must allow for several factors in the account, while also respecting the fact that the sergeant actually faced the FG 42 in combat, which cannot be said of this author. The FG 42 would remain a relatively uncommon weapon on the battlefield, and hence it was more liable to gather notoriety by its absence, and thereby generate fear when encountered. There is the distinct possibility, after all, that the US unit's encounter would have had just such serious consequences had the German unit been armed with an MG 34 or MG 42 plus the conventional mix of Wehrmacht small arms – other US after-action reports give similar losses without the presence of an FG 42. Yet the point that the Germans retreated 'not being held up by the weight of a larger machine gun' is valid. A medium machine gun like an MG 42 requires a team of supporting personnel rather than a single individual, and features accessories such as tripods, spare barrels, ammunition boxes, separate sights and range-finding devices. Everything to do with the FG 42, by contrast, could be carried by a single man.

In assessing the FG 42, therefore, we can say is that it was a qualified success. It was a fine semi-auto rifle, although its eventual weight must have been a burden for the soldier carrying it (the FG 42/II weighed 6.65kg, as against the 3.9kg of the Kar 98k). As a tactical machine gun, it ran into some of the same problems as the American Browning Automatic Rifle, firing an undoubtedly powerful cartridge from a limited ammunition supply (both used 20-round box magazines). Yet while this situation was not perfect, it seems beyond question that those units equipped with the FG 42 certainly had increased firepower over those that didn't. Ultimately, it may well be the case that production of the FG 42 was so limited that we are unable to gain a true picture of its value in combat. Had the original dreams of production runs in the hundreds of thousands come true, the experience for the Allied soldier on the front line may well have been even more harrowing than it was.

THE STURMGEWEHR IN COMBAT

The Sturmgewehr was, in many ways, a very different animal from the FG 42. (Note that from this point the term 'Sturmgewehr' will act as shorthand for the MP 43/MP 44/StG 44 series.) With its intermediate-power cartridge, it occupied a different slot in the spectrum of German firepower, and didn't have the demands of the light machine gun role placed upon it. As we shall see, the Sturmgewehr attracted all manner of experimental modifications and accessories throughout the war, some of them outlandish in nature. First, however, it is illuminating to reflect upon the gun's general performance in combat, to judge the extent to which it broke the mould in firearms design and proved the assault-rifle concept.

A useful way into this topic is once again to look at US military appraisals of the rifle, this time from the War Department's *Tactical and Technical Trends* series. The following report was published in April 1945, by which time the Sturmgewehr had been in circulation for some time.

A German mountain unit goes into action, probably in Italy in 1944. Revealingly, the whole unit is armed with StG 44 rifles, clearly illustrating how the Sturmgewehr was considered as a possibility for general issue. (Cody Images)

The account is worth quoting in full, as it lays the groundwork for much subsequent discussion.

In their attempts to produce a light, accurate weapon having considerable fire power by mass production methods, however, the Germans encountered difficulties which have seriously limited the effectiveness of the Sturmgewehr. Because it is largely constructed of cheap stampings, it dents easily and therefore is subject to jamming. Although provision is made for both full automatic and semiautomatic fire, the piece is incapable of sustained firing and official German directives have ordered troops to use it only as a semiautomatic weapon. In emergencies, however, soldiers are permitted full automatic fire in two- to three-round bursts. The possibilities of cannibalization appear to have been overlooked and its general construction is such that it may have been intended to be an expendable weapon and to be thrown aside in combat if the individual finds himself unable to maintain it properly.

The incorporation of the full automatic feature is responsible for a substantial portion of the weight of the weapon, which is 12 pounds [5.4kg] with a full magazine. Since this feature is ineffectual for all practical purposes, the additional weight only serves to place the Sturmgewehr at a disadvantage in comparison to the U.S. carbine which is almost 50 percent lighter.

The receiver, frame, gas cylinder, jacket, and front sight hood are all made from steel stampings. Since all pins in the trigger mechanism are riveted in place, it cannot be disassembled; if repair is required, a whole new trigger assembly must be inserted. Only the gas piston assembly, bolt, hammer, barrel, gas cylinder, nut on the front of the barrel, and the magazine are machined parts. The stock and band grip are constructed of cheap, roughly finished wood and, being fixed, make the piece unhandy compared to the submachine guns with their folding stocks.

The curved magazine, mounted below the receiver, carries 30 rounds of 7.92-mm necked-down ammunition. The rounds are manufactured with steel cases rather than brass; inside the case is a lead sleeve surrounding a steel core. With an indicated muzzle velocity of approximately 2,250 feet per second [76.2m/sec] and a boat-tail bullet, accuracy of the Sturmgewehr is excellent for a weapon of its type. Its effective range is about 400 yards [366m], although the Germans claim in their operating manual that the normal effective range is about 650 yards [594m]. The leaf sight is graduated up to 800 meters (872 yards). (US War Dept 1945)

All told, this assessment of the Sturmgewehr is largely negative. The first paragraph contains the most crucial views. While acknowledging the weapon's lightness and accuracy, the author of the report states that the poor production quality of the weapon severely limits its usefulness, being particularly susceptible to battle damage. Such is the author's low opinion of the Sturmgewehr that he even considers the possibility that it may have been regarded as 'disposable' once it had succumbed to mechanical failure. He also gives intelligence stating that German soldiers have been told to avoid full-auto fire unless in extremis, the weapon being 'incapable of sustained firing' (exactly what constitutes 'sustained' is not fully defined).

A German infantry unit stops for a rest amid the snows of Russia, 1944. The soldier taking a nap has a Gew 43, while his comrade immediately to his left has an StG 44 – two very different types of firepower. (BArch, Bild 101I-090-3912-19A, Etzhold)

Assessing the validity of these claims is complicated by the passage of time. More information about the individual weapon or weapons tested is required before we could truly use the above report to make a representative judgement over the entire Sturmgewehr series. There is also the distinct possibility of jealousy creeping in here; the author almost implicitly suggests that the M1 Carbine is a superior weapon (at least in terms of weight), while neatly avoiding the battlefield criticisms of the M1's insufficient stopping power and penetration, courtesy of a light .30-calibre round.

It would certainly be fair to accept that many late-war Sturmgewehr weapons suffered from poor production quality, as by the end of 1944 this problem was affecting many areas of German war manufacturing. The annual output of Sturmgewehr broke down as follows: 1943 – 19,501; 1944 – 281,860; 1945 – 124,616. Although German war production figures peaked in 1944 across almost all

Two German infantrymen on the Eastern Front man a defensive position with their MP 43/1s, which together could produce a hail of 7.92mm fire over an effective range of up to 400m. Two Model 1924 *Stielhandgranaten* (stick grenades) rest at the ready in front of the soldiers. (Cody Images)

areas of matériel, there is no doubt that the weapons being received at the front line from this year onwards often suffered from quality issues. Decent metals and woods were in increasingly short supply, and manufacturing processes were often affected by the intensifying storm of the Allied strategic bombing campaign. Therefore there must have been some significant variations in the weapons received by front-line soldiers, which in turn could account for individual reliability problems. We know, for example, that many late-war Sturmgewehr had poor-quality protective finishes to their metalwork, making them more prone to rusting and pitting, and therefore to jamming.

Yet the scale of the report's criticisms does not tally with our overall knowledge of the Sturmgewehr's capabilities and strengths. Trial feedback, for example, indicates that the Sturmgewehr performed well, certainly no worse than most other weapons put through the demands of the battlefield. A Luftwaffe assessment of the MP 43/1 in 1943, for example, compared the Sturmgewehr directly against the air force's own FG 42. In light of the fact that the Luftwaffe was at this point committed to go ahead with the FG 42, we might expect some nit-picking criticism. The report, however, largely gives the Sturmgewehr a solid endorsement. The following are key points:

- The MP 43/1 is of basic construction, readily understood, and functions without problems.
- Cartridge feeding is satisfactory and stopping or jamming has not occurred. Case ejection is to the right and does not impede the activity of others nearby.
- Ballistic performance out to 300 meters can be considered equal to the FG 42, K98k, and the self-loading rifles, but by 400 meters is noticeably less than others.

- Compared to the FG 42 it has a much slower rate of fire but the reduced recoil allows bursts of automatic fire to be accurate out to 300 meters. At this range, shot dispersion is considered to be excessive. (Quoted in Senich 1987: 68)

This assessment of the Sturmgewehr has a rather more authoritative feel than the US Army bulletin quoted above, not least because it gives specifics of performance based on trial standards. Jamming is not noted as a problem, nor is the weapon's capability to deliver full-auto fire. In fact, the US claim that Sturmgewehr-issued troops had to avoid full-auto fire was likely to have been the result of ammunition shortages rather than technical issues with the weapon. Furthermore, late-war ammunition for the Sturmgewehr was often of a lacquered-steel variety that could be brittle (steel was much cheaper to use than brass); split cases failing to extract was a frequent cause of the Sturmgewehr jamming, rather than the design of the gun itself.

Many postwar evaluations of the Sturmgewehr have also supported the gun's essentially sound design. Ownership of wartime Sturmgewehr weapons is far from uncommon in the United States, for example, and the internet is replete with uploaded videos of users firing the gun on full-auto without any problems, albeit in ideal conditions. The Sturmgewehr was

German paras ride into combat atop a Tiger tank, armed with StG 44 weapons. They are heading into action in the Ardennes offensive in the winter of 1944; the StG 44s proved well suited to combat in the short to medium ranges of the Ardennes forest. (Cody Images)

one of the weapons test-fired by Robert Bruce for his excellent book *German Automatic Weapons of World War II*, and his observations are enlightening. (Bruce's book is recommended for revealing accounts of modern firing trials of many German automatic weapons.) Firing the weapon – crucially a 1945 production model – in semi-auto mode, the Sturmgewehr proved to be both controllable and accurate as expected, with little recoil and 'negligible' muzzle jump, although accuracy deteriorated as the speed of semi-auto fire was increased. Full-auto fire brought a jam after a few bursts: a split case had stuck in the chamber and failed to extract. Indeed, of the several jams experienced during the day's firing, almost all were due to the quality of the ammunition, and Bruce also observed that the lacquer from the cartridges built up significantly in the chamber, and had to be laboriously removed.

Despite the problems with ammunition, and the vintage of the weapon, the Sturmgewehr tested by Bruce nevertheless performed well, as shown by this description of the weapons when used in assault-type firing:

> After refilling magazines we decided to fire in a variety of 'assault' stances, including hip and shoulder fire from kneeling and standing positions. All were accomplished quite naturally and efficiently, attesting to the weapon's excellent ergonomics. While semi-auto fire is, of course, the most accurate, short full-auto bursts were found to be impressively controllable. This held true not only for aimed shoulder fire, but also when snap shooting from the hip. (Bruce 2010: 113)

Here we see the balance and firepower of the Sturmgewehr in its classically conceived assault mode. The trial found the weapon less satisfying when firing from the prone position, on account of the long, curved 30-round magazine projecting from the bottom of the gun, forcing the weapon

This useful comparative photograph shows the relative sizes of (from bottom to top) the StG 44, the Soviet PPSh-41 submachine gun and the US M1 Garand rifle. (Phanatic)

away from the ground. Wehrmacht advice to combat soldiers was to scrape a shallow hole in the ground in which the magazine would sit, and further act as a monopod rest to aid stability. Bruce found this solution to be less than satisfactory, and better accuracy results were obtained by resting the barrel on a support rather than relying on the magazine as a monopod arrangement. Yet notwithstanding this issue, the reasons Bruce gives for the essential controllability of the Sturmgewehr can be summarized as follows:

A group of camouflaged German ski troops conduct a patrol in the winter landscape of Russia with their StG 44s. Note how the soldier in the centre of the picture is using his ski poles as an improvised gun mount. (Claus Espeholt)

- The weapon's substantial weight, combined with low-power ammunition.
- The front-heavy in-line configuration, which helps to control recoil and reduce muzzle climb.
- The 'linear recoiling mass' by virtue of the straight-in-line design and the gas piston positioned above the barrel.
- The ergonomic sense of the pistol grip and buttstock.

From Wehrmacht trials and from modern-day experience, we can conclude that the US Army's vocal criticism of the Sturmgewehr is largely unfounded, with ammunition more to blame for reliability issues. (The US Army experienced exactly the same problem when the M16 rifle was first issued to combat units in Vietnam during the 1960s.) Certainly the production figures for the Sturmgewehr were not insignificant, and it is unlikely that output would have increased so significantly in 1944 had the Wehrmacht been receiving a constant flow of adverse reports from the battlefield.

Actual combat accounts of the Sturmgewehr in action are, unfortunately, few and far between. The weapons were distributed mainly to infantry, Panzergrenadier and Waffen-SS units, some of the first MKb 42s going to 5. SS-Panzergrenadier-Division 'Wiking' in the spring of 1943. The actual levels of distribution varied according to the restrictions of logistics and supply. The commonly held belief that elite Waffen-SS units were given preference in terms of Sturmgewehr allocation does not hold water; Heer units were equal beneficiaries. If we take the case of Panzergrenadier companies in 1944 and 1945, for example, we see instances of entire platoons being armed with the StG 44. This distribution shows perfect fulfilment of the Sturmgewehr concept – its intermediate cartridge enabled it to replace both the Kar 98k and the MP 40 submachine gun within the platoon. Allied with the MG 42 for heavier fire support, the Sturmgewehr-armed platoons must have been able to generate devastating firepower over medium ranges. Furthermore, unlike the FG 42 the Sturmgewehr was not working within the limitations of a 20-round magazine, instead having 30 rounds in the staggered double-column magazine. A canvas-and-leather three-magazine pouch provided a practical piece of equipment for quick magazine changes. (A total of six magazines were provided with each gun, giving the soldier a total magazine-loaded supply of 180 rounds.) Field stripping and cleaning the Sturmgewehr was a relatively easy process, and as long as the soldier kept the weapon clean and properly oiled it would generally offer reliable service. Used within its optimum range limits – up to 400m – the Sturmgewehr was a sound weapon.

Sturmgewehr accessories and development

One element of the German war effort that attracts a mix of both admiration and pity was its near-inexhaustible desire for experimentation, even as the Reich itself crumbled into defeat. The Sturmgewehr was a case in point, as its already considerable degree of innovation attracted a wide range of accessories and tools, some of futuristic or outlandish design.

As early as late 1942, the Heer high command was proposing equipping MKb weapons with telescopic sights, and sights were later applied to some trials of MP 43/44 weapons. Typically these sights were the 1.5× Zf 41 or the 4× Zf 4. Given the capabilities of the *kurz* round, the fitting of telescopic sights was questionable at the outset. (The adjustable rear sight was graduated implausibly out to 800m in 100m increments, although a late-war modification seems to have reduced the maximum range to 400m, in 50m increments.) Reality also proved the optical sight unsuited to the Sturmgewehr. During trials it was found that just a magazine's worth of full-auto fire totally disrupted the sight's zero, and investment in improved mounts was deemed not worth the effort, given the fact that the Kar 98k was a far better 'scoped sniper weapon. The Luftwaffe comparative trials mentioned earlier verified this point by testing a Sturmgewehr fitted with a telescopic sight: 'A telescopic sight has proved of little value. At the established battle range of 300 meters, targets can be defined and hit with little difficulty by means of the tangent rear sight. Over 300 meters shot dispersion is excessive and penetration inadequate for sharpshooting purposes' (Quoted in Senich 1987: 68).

A more unusual, albeit forward-looking, sight experiment was the use of the Sturmgewehr with the Zielgerät 1229 (ZG 1229) active infrared device – known as the 'Vampir' (Vampire) – one of the first generation of night-vision weapon 'scopes ever used. This extremely bulky device was developed by C.G. Haenel, and consisted of an infrared spotlight set above an infrared-receptive 'scope, the power supply to the 'scope and searchlight provided by dedicated battery packs. The total weight of the whole system was more than 15kg, making the assault rifle a less than portable prospect on the battlefield. Nevertheless, the system did work, and very small numbers were used in combat on the Eastern Front in 1945, although to what effect is unclear.

Beyond the ZG 1229, the most imaginative modification of the Sturmgewehr was undeniably the special curved barrels and sight attachments, designed to allow the gun's operator to shoot around corners or around the blind angles of an armoured vehicle without revealing himself. Known collectively as the *Krummlauf* attachments, development of the devices began at Rheinmetall in late 1943, in response to a War Department directive. Two versions were produced – the *Vorsatz J* for infantry and the *Vorsatz Pz* for armoured use; it should be noted that these devices were initially developed primarily for the MG 34, hence the armoured application. Tests with the 7.92×57mm MG 34 proved the application to be a non-starter – the round was simply too powerful for the curved barrel – so eyes fell upon the reduced-power 7.92×33mm as an alternative. A demonstration in July 1944 of a Sturmgewehr fitted with a

A close-up of the *Vorsatz J* device, showing the prismatic aiming device from the rear. Once fitted to an StG 44, the *Vorsatz J* fundamentally unbalanced the weapon, and critically weakened the barrel after firing a few hundred rounds. (Cody Images)

90-degree curved barrel impressed a group of watching officers sufficiently to merit further development – the shots were grouped in a 30cm square at 100m. The 90-degree angle was soon deemed unnecessary for infantry use, so a 30-degree curve instead became the focus for the companies involved in the project: Rheinmetall, Bush, Zeiss and Bergmann. Sighting the weapon was an obvious challenge, and the problem was solved by various prismatic and mirrored sighting devices. The combined barrel/sight fitted onto the Sturmgewehr in a similar manner to attaching the weapon's grenade launcher, but the balance of the gun was affected dramatically; with up to 2kg of extra weight at the end of the gun, the shooter could only use the *Vorsatz* device when shooting the Sturmgewehr from the hip.

Further testing of four *Vorsatz* options continued at the Infanterie-Schule at Döberitz in November 1944, but none lived up to expectations. Barrel life was poor, accuracy was somewhat haphazard and recoil could be vicious – during some tests the actual barrel of the gun was torn off after 170 rounds of fire. Testing and trials continued into early 1945, and photographic evidence even shows that some of the devices received combat testing, but ultimately no more than a few hundred of these impractical devices were made by the end of the war.

The desire to shoot from a protected position was not only expressed through the *Vorsatz J* device. At around the same time as the curved barrels were being developed, a more mechanical solution for the protected shooter was emerging, in the form of the Deckungszielgerät. This was, in essence, a mechanical extension of the stock and trigger mechanism, into which the gun was fitted, and thereby enabled the soldier to fire the weapon via a transfer trigger. The sighting device consisted of two mirrors, arranged much like the periscope devices used for safe viewing over the parapets of trenches. Only 20 of these mechanisms were produced, and as far as we know none went into actual combat.

German experimentalism with the Sturmgewehr went well beyond external attachments, and in the last years of the war branched out into some more substantial redesigns of the weapon itself. A Sonderkommission Infanteriewaffen (Special Committee on Infantry Weapons), first convened in Berlin in July 1944, attempted to rationalize some of the many experimental small-arms programmes under way at the time. Among these were various redesigns of the Sturmgewehr, often with the goal of simplifying the weapon further for mass production. The complexities of these redesigns are too extensive to go into in detail here, but some selected examples are illustrative.

Großfuss created an extremely simple assault rifle based on the rough configuration of the Sturmgewehr, but operating on a fixed barrel with the gas imposing a delay on the opening of the breech mechanism. A single prototype was produced. Gustloff, meanwhile, produced two gas-retarded weapons known as the Models 507 and 508, essentially blowback-type guns of astonishing cheapness – the Model 507 even lacked a pistol grip. Mauser made prototypes of what was termed the Gerät 06. This used a roller-locked retarded blowback action, the simplified mechanism producing a weight saving of nearly 2kg compared to the standard Sturmgewehr. It also responded to the problem of the brittle steel 7.92mm *kurz* cartridge casings by featuring a fluted chamber, which helped prevent the case sticking to the chamber walls, and therefore aided smooth extraction of the spent case. The new gun was seen as a possible next step in the evolution of the Sturmgewehr – the MP 45 – but the realities of the wartime situation, and the impossibility of retooling under these conditions, meant that it did not reach a substantially developed form by the end of the war in May 1945.

A US Army officer handles an StG 44 fitted with a *Vorsatz J* curved-barrel device. This particular barrel describes a 90-degree angle, although the German weapons engineers eventually found a 30-degree angle to be optimal. (Cody Images)

IMPACT
Influence in defeat

The journey we have taken with German automatic rifles is undoubtedly one of impressive innovation and real engineering achievement. In the case of the Sturmgewehr in particular, we sense that had the war continued for a few more years, and had production conditions been rationalized in Nazi Germany, the Heer and Waffen-SS could have taken a definite firepower advantage on the battlefield. Had the common German soldier been armed with a Sturmgewehr or even an FG 42, the outcome of thousands of individual infantry battles might have been quite different. Only the timely conclusion of the war prevented us from seeing that possibility emerge.

The life of the German automatic rifles, however, did not stop conclusively with the end of hostilities in Europe. The active life of the Gew 41 and 43 largely stopped in 1945, limited by issues of long-term mechanical reliability. They have since become valued collector's items with firearms enthusiasts and historians. A quick glance on the internet at the time of writing revealed several Gew 43s for sale in the United States, selling in the region of US $2,500–3,000. The scarcer Gew 41 is currently commanding prices exceeding $5,000 depending upon the general quality of what is being sold. It is worth noting, however, that Brazil produced a .30-06 version of the Gew 43 – the Itajubá Model 954 Mosquetão – in the immediate postwar years.

When we turn to the FG 42 and Sturmgewehr, however, their significance for the future of firearms design was seminal. Looking first at the FG 42, the weapon itself was not adopted or manufactured officially by any state following the end of the war. Yet as modern states' militaries thought about the future of their infantry weapons, the design innovations

of the FG 42 – particularly its straight-in-line layout – could not be ignored. In Switzerland, W+F Bern and SIG both produced Sturmgewehr-labelled weapons in the 1950s that were to varying degrees indebted to the FG 42. W+F Bern's Sturmgewehr 52 (STG 52), for example, adopted a similar layout to the FG 42, the gun featuring a straight-in-line profile and a side-mounted magazine. It fired the 7.5mm *Kurzpatrone* round or, as the STG 54, the 7.5×55mm Swiss cartridge. SIG's SG 510/STGW 57 also had a similar flat profile along barrel, receiver and stock, although this gun worked on a roller-delayed blowback principle and had its magazine mounted conventionally beneath the receiver, just in front of the trigger guard.

The Gew 43, as with all other wartime German semi- and full-auto rifles, represents the gradual break from the bolt-action rifle as the standard infantry weapon during the middle years of the 20th century. (Joseph Magers)

Some of the most interesting developments of the FG 42 occurred well away from Europe, in the United States. When the first examples of the FG 42 were captured by US forces in World War II, the US ordnance authorities became fascinated by its general-purpose tactical concept. The chief of US Army Ordnance research and development, Colonel René R. Studler, ordered a study using three examples of the FG 42 as the foundation of a new US Army machine gun. The resulting weapon was the 7.92mm Light Automatic Machine Gun T44. The FG 42 outline was unmistakable, but to overcome the inadequacies of the 20-round magazine the FG 42's gas-operated mechanism was married to the belt-feed mechanism of the MG 42.

This experimental weapon was far from perfect. The light barrel, for example, overheated quickly when delivering sustained fire. Yet the intrinsic stability of the FG 42, particularly when fitted with a new muzzle brake, meant that the T44 was an accurate weapon, and could even be fired in the controlled manner from the shoulder or the hip. In this way the T44 laid the foundations for what eventually became the 7.62×51mm NATO M60 machine gun, the US Army and Marine Corps' primary medium machine gun from the late 1950s until the 1990s, although variants remain in service today. The M60 had a somewhat troubled existence, design flaws leading to its unflattering nickname – 'the Pig' – but its indebtedness to the FG 42 proves the German weapon's worth, and illustrates yet again how German wartime innovation, often conducted under the most pressing of circumstances, inspired postwar weapons design.

Nowhere is this truer than in the case of the StG 44. The inspiration in its design, and the numbers produced, ensured that it continued in service both in Germany and further afield. It was taken as a standard weapon of the East German Volkspolizei and the Nationale Volksarmee. A photo of a Volkspolizei parade in Neustrelitz in 1955 shows each of the

7 October 1955. A parade of East German Volkspolizei shows the StG 44 still in use a decade after the end of World War II. The Sturmgewehr weapons were retired from this service during the 1960s. (BArch, Bild 183-33349-0002, Löwe)

numerous officers clutching a Sturmgewehr across his chest, and the StG 44 would remain a police-issue weapon until 1962, when it was replaced with the PPSh-41 submachine gun. The Volksarmee, by contrast, swapped their MPi.44s (as the Sturmgewehr was relabelled) for the new AK-47 in the 1950s. (For more about the relationship between the AK-47 and the Sturmgewehr, see below.)

Further afield, the Sturmgewehr went on to serve in far-flung corners of the globe, via the circuitous supply routes that proliferated during the Cold War. The forces of both the Czechoslovak Socialist Republic and the Socialist Federal Republic of Yugoslavia utilized wartime stocks of the Sturmgewehr, the latter as late as the 1980s in airborne service. During the 1970s and 1980s, however, many Eastern Bloc countries (by now fully equipped with the AK-47) began either to pass over their Sturmgewehr rifles to reserve forces, or sell them off to ideologically aligned foreign buyers. In the Middle East, therefore, Sturmgewehr rifles have appeared in the hands of the Palestine Liberation Organization (PLO) and in those of gunmen on the streets of the Lebanon. (The latter have been witnessed as late as 2007.) Other specimens have cropped up in sub-Saharan Africa, and some were used by the communist insurgents in Vietnam during the wars of the 1940s–1970s. Other countries toyed with more legitimate options. Argentina's CITEFA concern, for example, even began producing its own versions of the StG 44 during trials in the late 1940s as a possible new infantry rifle. In the mid-1950s, however, the Argentinean armed forces opted instead to adopt the 7.62×51mm FN FAL.

If we broaden our perspective to consider the influence of the Sturmgewehr on the subsequent development of small arms, then it potentially becomes one of the most important weapons of the 20th century. For the StG 44 introduced the world to the concept of the assault rifle, an automatic weapon firing an intermediate cartridge over practical combat ranges. Within only a few years of the end of the war, the Soviets had adopted Mikhail Kalashnikov's AK-47 as the standard assault rifle of the Soviet forces. Not only was the layout of the AK-47 strikingly similar to that of the Sturmgewehr, with its top-mounted gas system and curved magazine, it also fired a new Soviet intermediate cartridge, the 7.62×39mm M43, developed by Soviet engineers Nikolay Elizarov and Pavel Ryanov during the mid-war years. The direct connection between the M43 and the German *Kurzpatrone* developed in the late 1930s has not been proved, but circumstantial evidence alone suggests a definite link, as firearms historian Gordon Rottman has pointed out:

> The Soviet designers were apparently familiar though with the 7.75×39mm Kurzpatrone developed by Gustav Genschow und Company A.G. (GECO) in Berlin-Treptow in 1934–35. There are too many coincidences for them not to have been. The Kurzpatrone and 7.62×39mm have the same case length, 1-to-20 ratio body taper, shoulder angle, head to shoulder distance, and caliber. The Germans measured caliber by the weapon's bore diameter and the Soviets by the bullet diameter, so the German 7.75mm round was actually 7.62mm. However, there is some debate as to whether the Russians had access to these rounds. (Rottman 2011: 12)

Whatever the connection between the M43 and the *Kurzpatrone*, what is certain is that the Soviets would have been aware of the assault-rifle concept by the late years of the war, having encountered and captured such weapons on the battlefield. Thus when engineer and soldier Mikhail Kalashnikov and others entered the race to design a new rifle for the postwar Red Army in the final year of World War II, it is scarcely conceivable that they were not aware of the Sturmgewehr. Kalashnikov himself, it should be noted, protests the inference:

> But Kalashnikov still insists, 'I didn't see captured German weapons. They were top secret. I was just a sergeant. How could I get access to them?' Perhaps Kalashnikov did not see an MP 43 although it seems unlikely that the major Russian weapons research and development centres in which he worked did not have supplies of the German weaponry for their designer technician to test. A captured StG 44 was

demonstrated at a meeting of the Soviet Arms Committee in 1943, and within six months two engineers, Nikolay Elizarov and Pavel Ryanov, had produced the 7.62×39mm cartridge. It was this intermediate cartridge that made Federov's dreams of a Russian assault rifle a reality; it only required someone to design that dream. (Hodges 2008)

Here Michael Hodges questions Kalashnikov's argument that his AK-47 design was wholly original. We must nevertheless recognize that the AK-47 contained much that was different from the Sturmgewehr, not least its rotating-bolt mechanism that gave the gun its awesome reliability. Furthermore, the AK-47 was a true gun for the everyman. When it finally emerged as the new standard Soviet Army rifle in the late 1940s, it began a revolution in global firepower. The AK-47 has literally shaped the nature of postwar conflict. With an estimated 100 million AKs (including all variants) manufactured to date, the AK has become history's most extensively distributed firearm (with catastrophic consequences for global security). In contrast to the German automatic weapons, which could be temperamental creatures when exposed to front-line conditions, the AK series was built with rugged reliability at its core. An ability to handle the ingress of dirt into the action (by virtue of relatively 'loose', and therefore forgiving, tolerances) and a simple gas mechanism have made a weapon of legendary toughness. A former officer with the Rhodesian African Rifles told the author that his patrol once came across an AK stuck in the mud of the Zambezi River, having spent six months under water before the dry season revealed it once again. (The officer knew the time interval because they had observed the weapons going into the water when they ambushed a group of insurgents six months previously, during the vicious Rhodesian bush war of the late 1970s.) One of the men in the patrol attempted to remove the magazine, but it had jammed fast into

This Syrian soldier, clad in a full chem-bio warfare suit, is armed with an AKM, a modernized version of the AK-47. Although the link between the AK-47 and the StG 44 is contested, the visual similarities alone suggest at least a general conceptual connection. (US Department of Defense)

place. Then, in an act of either total trust or bush madness, the soldier set the selector switch to full-auto, held the gun at arm's length and pulled the trigger. The AK fired all 30 rounds without stopping, in what must be the ultimate demonstration of a gun's reliability.

Exactly what the Sturmgewehr brought to this story is uncertain, but it is hard to conceive of the AK-47 without the StG 44 providing the foundations – not that everyone bought into the intermediate-cartridge concept straight away. The saga of postwar NATO ammunition standardization is truly a tale to be told, and only a skeleton outline of this history is possible here. In US forces, the superior qualities of the Garand meant that it continued to give stalwart service, including throughout the Korean War of 1950–53. By the mid-1950s, however, the weapon was undoubtedly beginning to show its age, not least as the AK-47 came into service with Soviet and Eastern Bloc forces. US troops became painfully aware of the Garand's now-inadequate magazine capacity of eight rounds, so the quest began to develop a new standard-issue firearm for American forces.

Intersecting with this development was experimentation with new types of cartridge for the next generation of Western rifles. The British in particular forged ahead with the intermediate-cartridge idea as they sought a replacement for the Lee-Enfield bolt-action rifle, which was now creaking with age. One of the early explorations was the EM2 rifle, a futuristic-looking bullpup weapon chambered for the British .280 cartridge (7.2×43mm). The performance of this gas-operated gun was respectable – it had a muzzle velocity of 771m/sec and an effective range of up to 700m. As with German thinking in relation to the Sturmgewehr, and Soviet thinking regarding the AK-47, the British wanted a weapon that could deliver controllable full-auto fire and which provided manageable performance characteristics over medium combat ranges. It was a promising way forward for the British, but now politics entered the fray. The formation of NATO in 1949 meant that some degree of equipment commonality and standardization between the armed forces of the member states was desirable. Yet there was

The M60 was a direct descendant of the FG 42. The intermediate step in its evolution was the T44, an experimental US weapon that brought together the gas system of the FG 42 and the belt feed of the MG 42. (US Department of Defense)

a battle of wills. The Americans – the strongest voice in the process – were resistant to the concept of the intermediate cartridge. They argued that while full-auto fire had its uses, it was typically a last resort, and semi-auto was more pragmatic on most occasions. Furthermore, a full-power rifle cartridge had, to US thinking, the broadest use across a wide spectrum of ranges. Not only could it guarantee substantial penetration of cover, but it could also deliver effective suppressive fire at ranges beyond 600m; US forces had a very strong marksmanship tradition, and US ordnance experts were concerned that adopting an intermediate cartridge

would limit the expression of that tradition. Counter-arguments about issues such as practical combat distances and the volumes of ammunition a soldier could carry largely fell on deaf ears. Defenders of the intermediate cartridge also pointed to the fact that the shorter case length involved meant that more compact weapons could be designed, improving the portability of small arms and their suitability for use by people with smaller physiques. Training times could also be reduced, as instructors wouldn't have to devote their efforts to teaching recruits how to handle heavy recoil.

While these arguments were rumbling on, the Americans had been developing a new cartridge for their future infantry weapons – the T65 – which had similar power and performance to the .30-06 round. The T65 round was an emphatic rejection of the intermediate-cartridge concept, and we probably can't discount the perceived 'manliness' of the new round as a factor in the US decision-making process. With a calibre of 7.62mm and a 51mm case length, the round developed a muzzle velocity in the region of 840m/sec and (depending on the weapon firing it) a killing range of up to and exceeding 1.5km.

After much debate and rancour, the United States got its way in terms of NATO standardization. The 7.62×51mm NATO became the official round of NATO forces, and most countries within the NATO remit therefore moved to adopt weapons that took the cartridge. The British, and eventually more than 90 other countries, adopted the Belgian FN FAL rifle; after the AK-47 the FAL is the most commercially successful postwar rifle. While the full-auto option was available for many variants of this weapon, the hefty kick of the 7.62mm NATO round meant that only the strong-willed or desperate tended to flick the selector to automatic. The British actually felt that the rifle was unsuited to full-auto fire, and so used a 'pure' semi-auto version, the L1A1 Self-Loading Rifle (SLR).

The FN FAL was undoubtedly a fine rifle, but the US authorities resisted its lure in preference for a home-produced weapon. This was the M14, essentially a modernized M1 Garand but with a 20-round magazine and a selective-fire capability. There was no doubting the solidity of the M14, and it was a dependable weapon for thousands of US soldiers from its introduction in 1959. Indeed, the qualities of the M14 have ensured that in some form or another it has survived to the present day, principally in accurized sniper formats such as the M21. Yet as a standardized infantry rifle the M14 had its problems. It weighed a ponderous 3.88kg (by comparison the later M16 weighed 2.86kg) and full-auto fire remained a bruising experience, in terms of recoil, ammunition consumption from the 20-round magazine and barrel overheating. For this reason, many M14s in service were fixed for semi-auto fire only. Furthermore, once M14s began to arrive with US soldiers in Vietnam, tactical issues began to emerge. The Viet Cong insurgents and regular North Vietnamese Army (NVA) soldiers could carry more ammunition into action than their US opponents, and their weapons were easier to handle in jungle combat, where the great range of the M14 proved largely irrelevant. (However, it was also found that the 7.62mm NATO rounds were somewhat better at punching through jungle foliage.) The controllable full-auto fire capabilities of the AK-47 also meant that on many occasions US troops found themselves unable to gain fire superiority,

A Spanish sailor here prepares his CETME rifle during an exercise. The rifle was designed by a German, Ludwig Vorgrimler, who worked for Mauser during the experimental latter years of World War II. (US Department of Defense)

particularly in close-range encounters. The M14's wooden furniture proved susceptible to the heat and humidity of the tropics, and distortions in the furniture resulted in problems with the gun's accuracy.

The solution to these problems lay, ironically, in a new gun and a new cartridge. Even as the M14 was being developed and the 7.62mm NATO round chosen, the aforementioned Colonel René Studler had commissioned studies into smaller-calibre weapons and their tactical applications on the battlefield. The conclusions of the research were largely the same as those Germans had come to in the 1930s, namely that a smaller round offered advantages in full-auto fire, recoil control, volume of ammunition carried and performance over practical combat ranges. (Obviously these results were ignored during the decision-making process regarding the 7.62mm NATO adoption.) For the purpose, engineers at the Aberdeen Proving Ground recommended a .22-calibre (5.56mm) round fired at extremely high velocities, and the great firearms designer Eugene Stoner eventually provided the weapon to take it – the .223-calibre Armalite AR-15. Compressing the story significantly, small numbers of AR-15s were filtered into US Air Force, US Marine Corps and US Army service in Vietnam, and despite some problems in the field the weapon was progressively adopted during the early 1960s, and M14 production was stopped in 1963.

The Mauser Gerät 06 was developed late in the war and was a possible successor to the StG 44. Although it didn't reach production status during World War II, its roller-delayed blowback mechanism influenced postwar rifle design. (Darkone)

In February 1967 the M16A1 became the standardized infantry rifle of the US armed services. Lightweight, gas operated, relatively compact (990mm long as opposed to the M14's 1,117mm), fast firing (800rpm) and with a small bullet delivered at 1,000m/sec, the M16A1 brought the true assault rifle into US hands. The volte face regarding the 7.62mm NATO calibre brought further acrimony among the NATO allies, but variants of the M16 have been carried by US soldiers to this day, and signs of a replacement are only now appearing after five decades of use. The British armed forces themselves eventually gave in to the inexorable shift towards the 5.56mm round, and in 1985 began replacing the FN FAL with the 5.56mm SA80. Other European and world armies made similar shifts, although 7.62mm NATO weapons remain in service in massive numbers around the world, and contribute to the still-vigorous debate about the best calibre for military use.

Looking back, we see the beginnings of this complex historical journey in Germany in the 1930s, when the Waffenamt began to engage seriously with issues of practical combat ranges, and their relationship to cartridge design. Weapons such as the Gew 41 and 43 contributed to the gradual shift from bolt-action to self-loading as the foundation of all postwar rifles. The FG 42 changed the game by offering a rifle that not only challenged notions about the very format of an infantry rifle, but also offered the possibility of a general-purpose weapon in the hands of a single individual. That theme has resurfaced in recent years with weapons such as the Mk 14 Enhanced Battle Rifle and the M27 Infantry Automatic Rifle (IAR), weapons purposely designed to shift between the close-quarters battle and support roles. The StG 44, depending on how the evidence is viewed, may have had an even more profound impact upon the general thread of small-arms development. Not only is it plausible that the gun influenced the creation of the greatest postwar firearm – the AK-47 – but it also had a direct bearing on the gradual shift towards the intermediate-calibre cartridge that now prevails in many of the world's standard-issue military rifles.

There are other threads of influence. The Gerät 06 – what was mooted as the MP 45 – was abortive in its own development, but its roller-locked delayed blowback action went on to inform the mechanisms of seminal weapons by Heckler & Koch (such as the G3 and its numerous variants and successors) and several rifles developed by the Spanish CETME company. Thus although we see many dead ends in German wartime rifle research, the fact remains that German automatic rifles laid foundations that are still visible in the world's firearms to this day.

CONCLUSION

It is ironic that the debate about the right type of cartridge for a military rifle is still continuing, and with some vigour. Even from the earliest days of the introduction of the 5.56mm round in Western service, there were some disquieting front-line reports of the small round delivering inadequate 'take-down' power, and of people surviving being struck by the 5.56mm when the .30-calibre or 7.62mm of the past would have been decisive. Many of the more anecdotal reports are informed by prejudice and myth. Soldiers can become keenly wedded to the weapon upon which they are trained and with which they fight, so often don't analyze a change in the most objective of terms. The accretion of more scientific analysis, however, does seem to show that cartridges such as the 5.56mm, especially when allied to short-barrelled carbines, truly don't have spectrum of ballistic performance needed for the modern battlefield, particularly with the widespread use of body armour.

For this reason, we are beginning to see new generations of cartridges being developed and tested, ones that give greater penetration and range without a punitive increase in the dimensions and weight of the cartridge. One such option is the 6.8mm Remington SPC, a round that sits somewhere between the 5.56mm and 7.62mm NATO. Some tests suggest that it delivers 40 per cent more penetrative energy than the current standard US M885 5.56mm round over 100–300m, and can extend the practical range of the rifle to 500m-plus. Evaluating the validity of these claims would take more space than is available here, but this debate is indicative of how firearms development is never set in stone, responding (often slowly) to the tactical and technical challenges of each new generation of battlefield conditions.

The German weapons we have studied here are perfect examples of this process in action. To their credit, German tacticians and military engineers honestly engaged with the realities of battlefield experience, using this knowledge to produce some of the most innovative weapons

German grenadiers advance across an open field near Aachen in December 1944. Two of the men boost the squad's firepower with StG 44s, while the other men are armed with Kar 98k rifles and (carried by the soldier at the front) a Panzerfaust anti-tank weapon. (BArch, Bild 183-J28344, Lohrer)

carried on the battlefields of World War II. To this day, weapons such as the FG 42 and the StG 44 appear truly modern in concept. Build the same weapons using modern materials, and some reasonably minor alterations to their inner workings, and they could take their place with confidence alongside many commercially available models. A cursory glance through YouTube shows many of these guns – principally the FG 42 and StG 44 – still burning through magazines at full-auto pace, doing exactly what they were designed to do more than 60 years ago.

Above all, the German automatic rifles demonstrate a *tactical* approach to weapons design. The Gew 41 and 43 were created to enhance the firepower of a single infantryman, multiplying his ability to put down accurate suppressive fire. The FG 42 was intended to give German airborne forces the edge during the first critical moments of a parachute or glider deployment, enabling them to switch between semi-auto precision and full-auto attrition simply by the flick of a selector switch and the deployment of a bipod. The Sturmgewehr weapons were designed to make soldiers enormously powerful within the actual ranges at which they fought, generating full-auto firepower that was controllable but which outstripped the performance of the submachine gun.

In many ways, these weapons achieved their goals. Some admittedly did not realize their full potential, but given time, further modifications and wider distribution their effects might now be written with more prominence in the history books. As it is, they gave the world a legacy of innovation that still influences the design of modern firearms.

GLOSSARY

BALL: A standard, inert military bullet type, typically of jacketed lead

BLOWBACK: A system of firearms operation that uses the breech pressure generated upon firing to operate the bolt

BOLT: The part of a firearm that closes the breech of the firearm and often performs the functions of loading, extraction and (via a firing pin) ignition

BREECH: The rear end of a gun barrel

BREECH-BLOCK: A mechanism designed to close the breech for firing; roughly analogous to 'bolt'

CARBINE: A shortened rifle

CARTRIDGE: A single unit of ammunition containing the bullet, propellant, primer and case

CHAMBER: The section at the rear of the barrel into which the cartridge is seated for firing

CLOSED BOLT: Refers to firearms in which the bolt/breech-block is closed up to the chamber before the trigger is pulled

COOK-OFF: The involuntary discharge of a cartridge by the build-up of heat in the chamber from firing

DELAYED BLOWBACK: A blowback mechanism in which the recoil of the bolt is mechanically delayed while the chamber pressures drop to safe levels

EJECTOR: The mechanism that throws an empty cartridge case clear of a gun following extraction from the chamber

EXTRACTOR: The mechanism that removes an empty cartridge case from the chamber after firing

GAS OPERATION: A system of operating the cycle of a firearm using gas tapped off from burning propellant

MOUNT: The physical means of attaching a telescopic sight to the body of a rifle

MUZZLE BRAKE: A device fitted to the muzzle of a large-calibre firearm, which deflects propellant gases to the side and rear and therefore helps reduce felt recoil

MUZZLE VELOCITY: The speed of the bullet as it leaves the muzzle of the gun. Note that the velocity of the bullet drops significantly once it has left the bore

OPEN BOLT: Refers to firearms in which the bolt/breech-block is held back from the breech before the trigger is pulled

RECEIVER: The main outer body of a gun, which holds the firearm's action

RECOIL OPERATED: An automatic weapon powered through the extraction, ejection and loading cycles by the forces of recoil. In a short-recoil weapon, the barrel and bolt recoil for less than the length of a cartridge before they unlock and ejection takes place

SEMI-AUTOMATIC: A weapon that fires one round and reloads ready for firing with every pull of the trigger

ZEROING: The process of ensuring that the point of aim indicated by the sights is the point at which the bullet will strike

Primary sources, printed and electronic

US War Department (1943). 'New German Semi-Automatic Rifle', *Tactical and Technical Trends*, No. 27, 17 June 1943 (http://www.lonesentry.com/articles/ttt07/german-semiautomatic-rifle.html, accessed on 22 August 2012)

US War Department (1944a). 'German Views on Use of the MG42', *Intelligence Bulletin*, Vol. II, No. 9, May 1944 (http://www.lonesentry.com/articles/intelligence-report/use-of-mg42.html, accessed on 22 August 2012)

US War Department (1944b). 'New German Rifle for Paratroopers', *Intelligence Bulletin*, June 1944 (http://www.lonesentry.com/articles/fg42/index.html accessed on 22 August 2012)

US War Department (1945). 'Machine Carbine Promoted – M.P. 43 Is Now "Assault Rifle 44"', *Tactical and Technical Trends*, No. 57, April 1945 (http://www.lonesentry.com/articles/ttt07/stg44-assault-rifle.html, accessed on 22 August 2012)

Secondary sources

Bruce, Robert (2010). *German Automatic Weapons of World War II*. Marlborough: Crowood Press Ltd.

de Vries, Guus (2012). *The FG42 Fallschirmjägergewehr*. Oosterbeek: Special Interest Publicaties BV.

de Vries, Guus & Martens, Bas (2003). *The MKb 42, MP43, MP44 and the Sturmgewehr 44*. Oosterbeek: Special Interest Publicaties BV.

Dugelby, Thomas & Stevens, R. Blake (1990). *Death from Above: The German FG42 Paratroop Rifle*. Cobourg: Collector Grade Publications.

Ford, Roger (1998). *The World's Great Rifles*. London: Brown Books.

Hodges, Michael (2008). *AK47: The Story of the People's Gun*. San Francisco, CA: Macadam/Cage.

Hogg, Ian (1996). *The Story of the Gun: From Matchlock to M16*. London: Boxtree Ltd.

Hogg, Ian (1999). *The Greenhill Military Small Arms Data Book*. London: Greenhill Books.

Hogg, Ian & Weeks, John (1991). *Military Small Arms of the 20th Century*. London: Arms & Armour Press.

Pegler, Martin (2006). *Out of Nowhere: A History of the Military Sniper*. Oxford: Osprey.

Rottman, Gordon L. (2011). *The AK-47: Kalashnikov-series Assault Rifles*. Oxford: Osprey.

Senich, Peter (1987). *The German Assault Rifle, 1935–1945*. Boulder, CO: Paladin Press.

Spooner, Russell (2005). *Seeking Signs of Sanity: A Veteran's Account of His Role in World War II*. Lincoln, NE: iUniverse, Inc.

Wacker, Albrecht (2005). *Sniper on the Eastern Front: The Memoirs of Sepp Allerberger, Knight's Cross*. London: Pen & Sword Military.

Walter, John (2004). *Guns of the Third Reich*. London: Greenhill Books.

Westwood, David. (2005). *Rifles: An Illustrated History Of Their Impact*. Santa Barbara, CA: ABC-CLIO

INDEX

Numbers in **bold** refer to illustrations.